NUNH
WITH PECKHAM RYE & NEIGHBOURHOOD

~ A historical guide and gazetteer ~

by Ron Woollacott

A Magdala Terrace, Nunhead,
Local History Publication
MMVIII

Copyright © Ron Woollacott

All rights reserved. No part of this publication may be reproduced
by any means without the permission of the publishers

First published May 2008

A Magdala Terrace, Nunhead
Local History Publication

Published by Maureen and Ron Woollacott
185 Gordon Road
LONDON SE15 3RT

ISBN 978-0-9526142-6-5

Maureen and Ron Woollacott are non-profit making self-publishers
of local history and related subjects, with the sole aim of promoting an
interest in our heritage and recording the past

Printed in England by the Catford Print Centre,
PO Box 563, Catford, London, SE6 4PY

ACKNOWLEDGEMENTS

It has been a labour of love reading the many books about the old Parish and Borough of Camberwell, including Nunhead and Peckham Rye, that have been written over the years in the compilation of this book, as well as delving into street directories and studying old maps going back 150 years or more. A list of some of the publications consulted will be found at the end of this book. I am particularly grateful to my daughter Mrs Michèle Louise Burford who has assisted me throughout the compilation of this book and helped solve some of the mysteries encountered along the way. Thanks also to Stephen G Priestley of Tappesfield Road for information about the early history of Nunhead. My thanks are also due to my dear wife and co-publisher Maureen for her patience and support. Maureen is a proud 'Nunhead Girl' having lived in Nunhead, and for a short while in Peckham Rye, all her life. Last but not least, I should also like to thank our friend, Mrs Min Surgison, another 'Nunhead Girl', for providing information about her brother, Mr Fred Shaw of Alderney, who was born in Barset Road Nunhead.

PICTURE CREDITS

The pictures on the following pages are from the collection of Michèle Burford and Ron Woollacott: front and back covers, pages 16, 27, 29, 32, 33, 36, 40, 47, 50, 55, 57, 58, 64, 66, 67, 68, 74, 78, 80, 87.

The photographs on the following pages are by the author: pages 15, 18, 19, 20, 21, 23, 24, 25, 26, 37, 38, 39, 41, 42, 44, 52, 53, 56, 59, 60, 61, 63, 70, 71, 73, 75, 76, 77, 79, 84, 88.

The photograph on page 86 is reproduced by permission of London Metropolitan Archives and the photograph on page 90 is by C Essex.

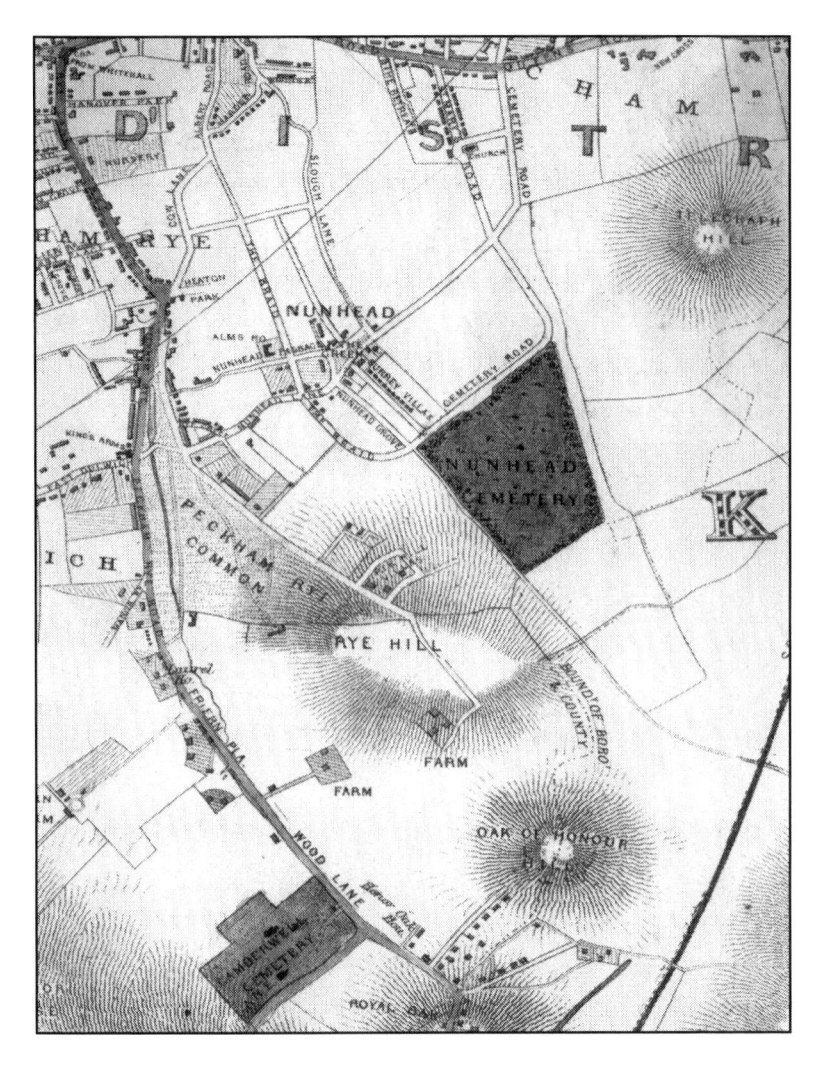

Nunhead and Peckham Rye 1857 (author's collection)

The *A-Z Master Atlas of Greater London* and similar street maps are recommended when using this gazetteer. Streets which no longer exist may be found in old street maps including *The A to Z of Victorian London,* Harry Margary 1987, *The A to Z of Edwardian London,* London Topographical Society, 2007, and *Old Ordnance Survey Maps,* in particular London sheets numbers 103, 104, 117, 118, published by Alan Godfrey Maps. www.alangodfreymaps.co.uk

INTRODUCTION

The districts of Nunhead and Peckham Rye in the London Borough of Southwark were once hamlets in the ancient parish of St Giles, Camberwell, in the County of Surrey, and at different times belonged to the Lords of the Manors of Bredinghurst, Camberwell Buckingham, Camberwell Fryern and Peckham.

With the setting up of the Metropolitan Board of Works in 1855 the ancient parish of Camberwell, which also included the former villages of Camberwell, Dulwich, Peckham and a part of the Manor of Hatcham, became a metropolitan district. Just 20 years later, the Camberwell historian, W H Blanch, wrote: *From a straggling suburban parish of about 4,000 inhabitants, Camberwell has become a congeries of streets, part of the great metropolis itself. Bricks and mortar, and universal stucco, have invaded the place, and green fields and hedge rows are fast deserting us.*

In 1856 the General Post Office (GPO) divided the metropolitan area into 10 postal districts: Camberwell and Dulwich were in the Southern district, and Peckham and Nunhead were in the South Eastern District. The Southern District was abolished in 1868 and Camberwell and Dulwich joined Peckham and Nunhead in the South Eastern District.

In 1888 the metropolitan parish of St. Giles, Camberwell was incorporated into the Administrative County of London, and in 1899 it became a metropolitan borough.

Numbered postal districts were first introduced by the GPO in 1917 during the First World War. Nunhead and Peckham Rye (east side) and Peckham Rye Common were allocated the London SE15 (Peckham) postal district, and Peckham Rye (west side) and Peckham Rye Park the SE22 (East Dulwich) postal district.

In 1965 the Metropolitan Borough of Camberwell was united with the Metropolitan Boroughs of Bermondsey and Southwark, to form the present London Borough of Southwark.

NUNHEAD

William Harnett Blanch, who amassed a large collection of original documents in the 19th century, discovered a deed proving that the name 'Nunhead' goes as far back as 1583. Nunhead is variously referred to in early maps and documents as lying in Surrey or Kent. It appears on John Rocque's map of 1745 as 'None-Head', when it consisted of a few cottages near the Nun's Head Tavern. The tavern was reputedly licensed in the reign of Henry VIII, according to a sign that could be seen on the 19th century building. A similar sign was placed on the front of the pub when it was rebuilt in 1934.

Nun's Heads make uncommon signs and usually denote a messuage (dwelling house). It was widely believed that the tavern covers the site of a convent or priory, but there is no evidence to support this theory.

In the early years of the 19th century the tiny hamlet was surrounded by arable fields, meadows and market gardens. A few cottages abutted the tavern together with a farm house, barns, and cattle sheds. A few houses had appeared on the main thoroughfare (Nunhead Lane) leading to Peckham Rye. The hamlet was connected to the main village of Peckham by Hook's Lane, later known as Slough Lane, which became Kirkwood Road. A track, which is now the busy Evelina Road, linked Nun Green to Hatcham (New Cross).

In 1815 an anonymous epicurean wrote: *From Peckham Rye, an excursion is frequently made to the Nun's Head, where a rural dinner, with vegetables fresh from the garden may be had in summer.*

The principle land owners in the 1830s were Charles Shard, who had inherited part of the Manor of Bredinghurst from his brother, including some land near Nun Green; Sir Thomas Smyth, Lord of the Manor of Camberwell Fryern, who owned most of the land west of present day Linden Grove; and Sir Claude Champion de Crespigny, whose property lay to the north of Nunhead Lane.

The several arable fields and meadows comprising Nunhead Hill belonged to William Warlters and Richard Edmonds of Hatcham. The Edmonds family were large landowners in Deptford and Camberwell and in 1804 purchased several plots of land at Nunhead and Peckham Rye from the Smyths.

In 1839 Edmonds and Warlters sold Nunhead Hill (about 130 acres) to the London Cemetery Company. About 52 acres were marked out for a cemetery, and the remaining acreage was sold to Henry Ewbank, a City merchant, of Denmark Hill, Camberwell. The cemetery was laid out in 1840, and this was followed by the appearance of several villas on the approach road to the cemetery.

The historian, Edward Wedlake Brayley, mentions a chapel associated with the Christian Instruction Society, being opened at Nun Green (now Nunhead Green) on the 8th June 1836.

The 1851 Post Office Directory for Surrey describes Nunhead as follows: *Nunhead, in the parish and union of Camberwell, in Brixton Hundred, one mile south-east from Peckham. Nunhead Cemetery is situated here upon a declivity; it is entered by a handsome iron gate, supported by appropriate lodges; the grounds are tastefully laid out, and in the centre, upon the highest part, is the chapel, which is chiefly built of stone. Here are almshouses for 7 aged people (called Beeston's gift), erected in 1834, by the Girdlers' Company, who are appointed trustees; also a neat chapel for the Independents.*

In 1850 the principal streets in Nunhead were Cemetery Road (now Linden Grove), Nunhead Lane, Nunhead Grove, and Nunhead Road, later renamed Albert Road and now Consort Road. Benjamin Trott was landlord of the Nun's Head Tavern, and there were just two shops in the hamlet, one of which was a grocery store. There were three preparatory schools run by ladies, and a gentlemen's boarding school.

Between the mid-1840s and 1850 several villas had appeared on that part of the approach road from Nunhead Lane to the cemetery, which was renamed Linden Grove. The Belvedere Tavern (recently demolished) was built at the corner of Linden Grove and Nunhead Grove in 1851.

By 1861 Gordon Road and Surrey Villas (now Banstead Street) had been laid out, but very few houses had been built.

In 1865 the railway came to Nunhead when the London, Chatham and Dover Railway Company opened a branch line from Cow Lane Junction, Peckham, to the Crystal Palace at Sydenham. Nunhead Junction Station opened in 1871. Several fields, between the railway embankment and what is now Kirkwood Road, were occupied by Charles Thomas Brock's firework manufactory.

By the mid-1870s most of the meadows and market gardens north of the cemetery had given way to brick fields and building lots. A local newspaper reporter described the scene in 1874 following a visit to Brock's factory: *Our notice is not intended to be topographical, or we might have had something to say concerning the venerable hamlet surrounding Nunhead Green, that has been the nucleus of the suburban district, now known as Nunhead. There is but little affinity or likeness between the ancient buildings in the neighbourhood of the pretty little green, and the rows of mushroom modern houses near them, some of which, door less and windowless, although somewhat aged as regards brickwork, are in the condition of undeveloped fungi.*

The 1874 Post Office Directory described Nunhead as: *A hamlet, in the liberty or district of Peckham, parish and union of Camberwell, Brix-*

ton Hundred, a mile and a half S W of New Cross Railway Station, 1 mile south from Peckham. The London, Chatham and Dover Railway has a station here. Here is the church of St. Michael. Sam Green, Postmaster, 2 York Place, Nunhead Green.

Practically the whole of Nunhead as far north as Lugard Road was built in the 1870s and 1880s and by 1890 the entire district, except for an area to the south of Nunhead, had been covered with streets, houses, shops, churches, chapels, public houses and factories. The population which in 1840 had been about 200 had grown to more than 10,000. In less than 50 years the sleepy Surrey hamlet had been transformed into a busy and densely populated suburb of south-east London.

By 1900 the gentry had moved away, and their houses were divided up and let to several families, converted into flats, or else acquired for commercial use. Between the two World Wars several fine Victorian villas in Linden Grove were demolished to make way for a London County Council housing estate, and during the Second World War much property was damaged or destroyed. Prefabricated bungalows, popularly known as 'prefabs', were built on cleared bomb sites.

After the war some rebuilding took place, but the greatest changes came in the 1960s and 1970s when many hundreds of Victorian houses, not all beyond repair, were bulldozed and replaced by large council estates. Fortunately, some of the old buildings, mainly at the centre of Nunhead, were retained and restored, mainly due to the efforts of the Nunhead Residents Association.

The ecclesiastical parish of Nunhead (formed 1990) incorporates the former separate parishes of St Antony and St Silas, Nunhead, and encompasses most of the streets lying between Brayards Road and Brenchley Gardens, including the Honor Oak Estate, Brockley (in the Borough of Lewisham), and part of Peckham Rye. A part of Nunhead is in the parish of St Mary Magdalene.

The modern district of Nunhead has no defined boundary. Generally speaking it is usually considered to comprise that part of the London Borough of Southwark which lies east of Peckham Rye, south of Peckham High Street and north of Honor Oak, with Nunhead Green somewhere in between.

PECKHAM RYE

Peckham Rye is shown on John Rocque's map of 1745 as several dwellings about one mile south of the village of Peckham, to which it is connected by a winding country lane, originally South Street, and now a busy cosmopolitan shopping street known as Rye Lane.

Peckham is mentioned in the Domesday Survey of 1086 where it is called Pecheham and held by Odo, Bishop of Bayeux. The origin of the name Peckham is obscure. Some etymologists say it means the village under the hill; Peckham sits below the hills of Nunhead, Hatcham and Honor Oak, while others suggest the name derives from 'Peche's home', Peche or Puck being a mischievous sprite.

The first mention of Peckham Rye is in the 14th century. The suffix 'Rye' is from an old English word meaning brook or stream. Peckham Rye began as a small settlement by a stream known as the River Peck at the northern end of Peckham Rye Common.

The author of *The Epicure's Almanack* (1815) recommended paying a visit to the White Horse at Peckham Rye: *This for a country tavern, is a very good one, and is often selected by parties from town as the scene of their banquets champêtres* (rural banquets).' He went on to suggest that patrons may, if so inclined after dinner, take a walk or ride up the common to Forest Hill: *The trouble of walking will be amply requited by the view which has recently been further embellished by the completion of the Croydon Canal* (now the Brockley railway cutting).

By the late 1820s, the weather-boarded cottages, mostly occupied by agricultural workers and labourers, had been joined by several substantial houses and stucco villas built to accommodate wealthy city merchants and their families who were moving into the area.

By the 1840s the White Horse Tavern had been joined by four more inns: the Rye House, the Lloyd's Head, the Green Dragon and King's Arms. George Creed operated a coach service from Peckham Rye to London, and James Prince and his four sons ran an omnibus service from the King's Arms to the City at a shilling fare.

Henry Drew, the landlord of the White Horse, ran an omnibus service to London in competition with Thomas Tilling, who had started his omnibus service from the Adam and Eve in Peckham High Street in 1851.

Gradually the market gardens and meadows surrounding Peckham Rye were replaced by new streets and houses, and the opening of Peckham Rye Railway Station in December 1865 encouraged further development.

In 1865 Sir William Bowyer Smyth, the Lord of the Manor, claimed absolute ownership of Peckham Rye Common and proposed building on it. The local folk objected and his claim was rejected by a committee of the House of Commons. In 1868 the manorial rights were purchased by the Vestry of Camberwell, and the common was saved as an open space for the people forever.

In 1890, Edwin Jones, joint-proprietor with George Randell Higgins of Jones and Higgins departmental store, Rye Lane, who was a member of the new London County Council, handed in a petition from the local inhabitants asking the Council to contribute towards the purchase of a plot of farmland adjoining Peckham Rye Common, as an extension to the common.

After much debate it was agreed that the grounds of Homestall Farm be acquired under the LCC General Powers Bill for 1891. Some properties, including an old farmhouse, were let on lease to the occupants. Originally known as the Peckham Rye Extension, the open space was formally opened as Peckham Rye Park on Whit Monday 1894.

Alfred and Charles Stevens were the last tenants of the farmhouse. Charles died in 1897, and following the death of his brother Alfred in 1906, the LCC took possession of the farmhouse and out-buildings in January 1907.

In July 1912, the north end of Peckham Rye was incorporated with Rye Lane and the Heaton Arms public house at No 1 Peckham Rye became No 249 Rye Lane.

Apart from some rebuilding, and the loss of many hundreds of mature trees in the drought of 1976 and great wind storm of 1987, the area looks much as it did at the turn of the last century. Recent losses include the old villa which was later used as the office of Deanes pram factory and the 1930s factory of Roberts Capsule.

In old documents Peckham Rye extends as far south as Honor Oak. Indeed, when Camberwell Parish Cemetery was laid out in Wood Lane (now Forest Hill Road) in 1856, it's address was 'Forest Hill, Peckham Rye, Surrey'.

Peckham Rye is shared by the parishes of St Antony with St Silas, and St John the Evangelist, Goose Green, East Dulwich.

Please note: Streets and buildings marked* no longer exist.

For more information about street names see *Origin of Names in Peckham and Nunhead* by John D Beasley; *Camberwell Place and Street Names and their Origin* by L S Sherwood; and *Lewisham Street Names and their Origins (before 1965)* by Joan Read.

ABBOTSBURY MEWS, NUNHEAD GROVE: A group of two-storey houses built 1989 on the site of the former Royale Pram Factory (Besfoldas Ltd) makers of 'The world's most beautiful baby coach.' Abbotsbury is a place in Dorset. (Beasley).

AJANTA HOMES, CONSORT ROAD: A large apartment block built for 'key workers' 2003-4 on the site of Victorian terraces and the 'Gold Diggers Arms' public house (q.v.).

*ALBION TERRACE, GORDON ROAD: A row of Gothic style almshouses built by the Metropolitan Beer and Wine Trade Society in 1872. The eight houses were originally let for the purpose of increasing the income of the Society, the ultimate aim being to open them for the admission of 16 more inmates. They were purchased by Southwark Council in the 1970s and demolished to make way for Barton Close (q.v.).

*ALEXANDRA HOTEL, GIBBON ROAD: A Victorian public house destroyed by a VI flying bomb during the Second World War. It stood at the corner of Gibbon Road and Senate Street and was known locally as 'The Alex'.

ALMOND CLOSE, ATWELL ESTATE: Named after the almond tree on the estate in association with Hazel Close c.1963. [Beasley].

ANSDELL ROAD: Laid out in 1872 and taken over as a new street by the Vestry of Camberwell in 1876. The houses were built by several speculative builders between 1873 and 1876. The first householders included: a schoolmaster, three lithographers, two telegraphers, a photographer, an army captain, and a master mariner. All were newcomers from outside the London area. Of around 90 houses built at least 18 remained uninhabited in 1881. In the 1940s and 1950s Nunhead Food Products, canned goods merchants, were based at No 82. The street may have been named after Richard Ansdell (1815-1885), animal painter. [Sherwood].

APEXX, No 138 GORDON ROAD: An apartment block consisting of 12 flats built on the site of Kemp's joinery works in 2007. The site was formerly occupied by a red pottery works in the 19th century.

AQUARIUS GOLF COURSE: See Beachcroft Reservoir. Sir Henry

Cotton (1907-87), the famous golfer, and his brother Leslie, became junior members of the club after the First World War and both won the club championship before reaching the age 13. Henry became a professional golfer at the age of 16.

ATHENLAY ROAD, WAVERLEY PARK: Laid out in the 1880s on Edward Yates's Waverley Park Estate (q.v.). Parts of this street were in the parish of Lewisham and were taken over as a new street by the Vestry of Lewisham between 1890 and 1899. The final section was taken over by the Metropolitan Borough of Lewisham in 1923. On the 15th October 1944 a VI flying bomb came down and destroyed many houses in Athenlay and Fernholme roads killing eight people.

*ATWELL ARMS, ATWELL STREET: A Victorian pub demolished in the 1960s to make way for the Atwell Council Estate.

ATWELL ESTATE, PECKHAM RYE: A low-rise housing estate built in the 1960s by Camberwell Borough Council on the site of Atwell Road, Atwell Street and Copeland Avenue.

*ATWELL ROAD AND STREET, PECKHAM RYE: Both streets were laid out in the 1860s. Atwell Street was adopted by the Vestry of Camberwell in 1866, and Atwell Road was taken over in 1874. In the 1880s the occupants were mainly carmen, coachmen, and construction workers. Both streets disappeared when the Atwell Estate (q.v.) was built in the 1960s. Possibly named after Hugh Atwell or Attawell, a member of Edward Alleyn's company in the 1600s. [Sherwood].

AURA COURT, PECKHAM RYE: Built on the site of Deane's pram factory demolished in 2005. Building commenced in 2006 and was completed in 2007. Deane and Co, makers of the Deanette bassinette, a luxury perambulator, is mentioned by Muriel Spark in her novel *The Ballad of Peckham Rye.* On top of the building was a giant baby carriage which was for many years a local landmark.

AUSTINS COURT, PECKHAM RYE: Built in 1996 on the site of Austin's second-hand furniture emporium which dominated this corner of Peckham Rye and Scylla Road for many years. G Austin and Son, became one of the largest antique furniture dealers in Europe. The firm was founded by George Austin (1845-1927), an Oxfordshire man, who came to London and opened a dairy at No 39 Brayards Road (q.v.) in the early 1860s. He later expanded into the removals and second-hand furniture business, and served on the Vestry of Camberwell from 1894 to 1900. He died at his residence 'The Anchorage', a large house which stood at the corner of Peckham Rye and Barry Road. He is buried in Nunhead Cemetery. The house was destroyed during the Second World War, and the site is now covered by Roy Brooks Estate Agency.

George Austin's Antique Emporium, Peckham Rye c.1973.
Austins Court, built 1996, now occupies the site.

BANFIELD ROAD: A private road, originally a driveway by the side of the former bus garage which led to the offices, paper mills and warehouses of Waxed-Papers Ltd (q.v.). It is named after Charles Banfield, who worked for the London General Bus Company at Nunhead, and later acquired the garage for his fleet of coaches. The garage was demolished in 1999 - together with the old paper mills - for a housing development. A replica clock tower was built on the site at the request of the Peckham Society, the amenity society for London SE15.

BANSTEAD STREET: Formerly Surrey Lane (1860s) leading to Surrey Villas and Surrey Square. Taken over as a new street by the Vestry of

Camberwell in 1883. In an attempt to reduce the number of 'Surreys' in local names, the Surrey village of Banstead was chosen as an alternative name. [Sherwood]. The section adjoining Nunhead Green was renamed Cheam Street in 1979 to continue the Surrey theme. On the 26th June 1944 a VI flying bomb came down killing one person and destroying several houses.

BARFORTH HALL, BARFORTH ROAD: Built as St Antholin's Church Hall on a garden site given in 1929 by George Augustus Holmes (1861-1943), organist and composer of many works for pianoforte, and author of preparatory manuals for piano and violin. He was sometime director of examinations at the London College of Music. In the 1930s many concerts were held here. Jack Warner (of Dixon of Dock Green fame) and his sisters, Elsie and Doris Waters, were just three of the many famous entertainers who performed on its stage. In the 1940s and 1950s it was a popular venue for dances, and during the 1970s several public meetings were held here pending redevelopment of the area. In the 1990s the Church of God in Calvary met here.

No 16 Barforth Road, Nunhead 1914

BARFORTH ROAD: Laid out in the late 1860s and adopted as a new street by the Vestry of Camberwell in 1881. The original occupants were lower middle-class and included a bank manager, a surveyor, and a spirit

merchant. Most were wealthy enough to employ a domestic servant.
The Revd John Chetwode Postans (1833-1905), minister of Linden Grove Congregational Church, lived at No 13 in the 1880s. His son, the Revd George Chetwode Postans, Congregational minister also lived here. He lived for a while at No 36 Rye Hill Park and at the time of his death resided at No 13 Tresco Road.

BARSET ROAD: The first houses were built by J Dadd of Cemetery Road between 1877 and 1881. The street was adopted by the Vestry of Camberwell in 1881. The first occupants were mainly working class folk.
Fred Shaw (1942 -), deep sea diver, was born at No 15 Barset Road (now demolished). He married an Alderney girl, and on moving to the island joined a salvage team. In 1972 he and another diver, Richard Keen, discovered the LSWR passenger steamer *Stella* which sank in 1899 with the loss of over 100 lives. He made a major contribution to marine archaeology in 1992 when he discovered an Elizabethan ship which was the subject of a major survey and film by Oxford University's diving team. Fred also took part in the filming. By 2000 he had dived on over 70 wrecks around Alderney. **Clive Jermain** (1966-88) lived in Barset Road. He found fame at the age of 20 when his play, *The Best Years of Your Life*, was shown on BBC TV in May 1986. Courageous Clive died of cancer of the spine just two years later.

BARTON CLOSE: An award winning low-rise housing development, built by Southwark Council on the site of Albion Terrace (q.v.) fronting Gordon Road, and the back gardens of the Beer and Wine Society's Homes, Nunhead Green. Work began in January 1976 and was completed in 1978. The architects were Myles and Deidre Dove. It is named after Elizabeth Barton, the Holy Maid of Kent, who was a nun during the reign of Henry VIII. She was executed at Tyburn in 1534 for predicting the king's death if he divorced Catherine of Aragon to marry Anne Boleyn. Jack Hallam, author of *The Ghosts' Who's Who* 1977, claims that Elizabeth Barton not only haunts the churchyard of Greyfriars in the City, where she is buried, but also appears as a faceless figure at Nunhead. There is no evidence to suggest she had any association with Nunhead.

BASSWOOD CLOSE: A small estate built in the late 1970s next to Citron Terrace (q.v.) on the site of No 1 Linden Grove. Basswood is a variety of linden tree. The Victorian villa was used by the Army Cadet Force and Territorial Army in the 1950s. The gate lodge (on Nunhead Lane) was occupied by Reginald Cutler, a confectioner, for many years.

BEACHCROFT RESERVOIR, NEWLANDS: Built on the site of Priory Farm and cricket fields and completed in 1909. It was opened by Sir George Truscott, Lord Mayor of London, and named after Sir Melvill Beachcroft, first chairman of the Metropolitan Water Board. The reservoir, hidden beneath the appropriately named Aquarius Golf Course (q.v.), holds 60 million gallons, and took 400 men three years to build. A masterpiece in 16 million bricks, it was once the world's biggest reservoir.

Beachcroft Covered Reservoir c.1973

*BEAUFORT HOUSE, PECKHAM RYE: Beaufort House was the home of Samuel Hulme Day (1805-76), a descendant of John Day, the Elizabethan printer. He was a wine merchant in the City of London, and a magistrate and Deputy Lieutenant for the County of Essex. His son, Lewis Foreman Day (1845-1910), artist and designer, and a founder of the Arts and Crafts Movement, was born at Rye Terrace, Peckham Rye. Beaufort House was pulled down in the 1930s, and replaced by Brookstone Court (q.v.).

BEAUFORT TERRACE, NUNHEAD LANE: A 19th century terrace destroyed by a VI flying bomb in 1944. Tilling House, built 1950, now occupies the site.

Dr Robert Bigsby FSA, FRS (1806-73), author, antiquary and collector, lived at No 4. He owned a large collection of ancient relics, including Sir Francis Drake's astrolabe and tobacco box. He presented the astrolabe to King William IV. **Sir James Augustus Henry Murray** (1837-1915) first editor of the Oxford English Dictionary, lived at No 6 in the 1860s when he was plain Mr Murray. His first wife, Maggie, died there in 1865 and was buried in Nunhead Cemetery. **Harold James Ruthven Murray** (1868-1955), chess historian, son of James Augustus Henry Murray and his second wife, Ada Agnes Ruthven, was born at No 6 Beaufort Terrace. In 1913 he published *A History of Chess*. He also contributed articles to the *British Chess Magazine*.

BEER AND WINE HOMES, NUNHEAD GREEN: Former almshouses belonging to the Metropolitan Beer and Wine Trades Society now owned by Southwark Council. A Gothic building, with tall chimneys set at odd angles, designed by William Webbe and built 1852-53. The foundation stone was laid by Lord Monteagle, the president of the society, on 9th June 1852. The Society's motto 'live and let live' is inscribed over the central archway which once led to the gardens now covered by Barton Close Estate (q.v.). Grand garden parties were held here in the 1960s.

Metropolitan Beer and Wine Homes awaiting refurbishment in 1975

BEESTON'S GIFT ALMSHOUSES, CONSORT ROAD: This is the oldest building in Nunhead. The terrace of seven stuccoed Tudor style almshouses was completed in 1834 to house poor members of the Girdlers' Company. Cuthbert Beeston was a Master of the Girdlers' Company and founded seven almshouses in the parish of St Olave, Southwark near London Bridge in 1582. The Girdlers' Company sold the site in the 1820s and the money was used to build the almshouses in Nunhead. The single storey wings were added in the late 1960s and reflect the style and design of the main terrace. The original building was restored, and with its modern additions won a Civic Trust Heritage Award in 1975. Another group of single storey buildings has been added bearing the name 'Palyns', which replace the almshouses of the same name in Choumert Road, Peckham, now owned by Southwark Council.

Beeston's Gift, Girdlers' Almshouses, Consort Road

BELFORT ROAD: Formerly Wellington Road. The name was changed in February 1938. Adopted as a new street by the Vestry of Camberwell in 1870. At the time of the 1881 census most of the householders were wealthy enough to employ a female domestic servant.

BELLWOOD ROAD, WAVERLEY PARK: Laid out in 1887 and adopted by Camberwell Borough Council in 1902. Possibly named after Bellwood, a seat in Midlothian, reminiscent of Sir Walter Scott's 'Waverley Novels'. [Sherwood].

BELVEDERE MEWS, NUNHEAD GROVE: A small housing unit dating from 1989, built at the rear of the 'Belvedere Tavern' on the site of a mission hall.

*BELVEDERE TAVERN, No 43 LINDEN GROVE: Built in 1851 in what was then Cemetery Road and is now Linden Grove. Belvedere means 'fair sight' in Italian, and the tavern was so-named because in days gone by the views from here were quite magnificent. There was a skittle alley at the rear of the tavern which became the site of the Cheltenham College mission hall in the late 19th century, and was afterwards used for commercial purposes. Belvedere Mews (q.v.) now occupies the site. The pub was demolished in 2005.

The Belvedere Tavern c.1972

BLACKPOOL ROAD: Laid out in the 1860s as Russell Road and adopted by the Vestry of Camberwell in 1869. Its name was changed to Blackpool Road in March 1938. The first occupants were labourers.

BORLAND ROAD, NEWLANDS: A part of this road was known as Marylebone Road until June 1891, and the section between Stuart Road and Brockley Footpath (next to Nunhead Cemetery) was called Arnold Road to 1901. Along with Sartor Road (q.v.), this was one of the first streets to be laid out in the Newlands area of Nunhead and Peckham Rye in the 1860s. Borland Road was taken over by the Vestry of Camberwell in 1890 and 1891 respectively. It is named after John Borland (1826-1896), a provision merchant and former vestryman of Camberwell, who took an active interest in the affairs of the parish, and was a churchwarden of St Giles, Camberwell and a governor of Wilson's Grammar School. Borland died at 111 Barry Road, East Dulwich, and was laid to rest in Camberwell Old Cemetery.

BOURNEMOUTH CLOSE: Part of the Atwell Estate (q.v.).

BOURNEMOUTH ROAD: Laid out in the 1860s and taken over by the Vestry of Camberwell as a new street in 1874.
> **Margaret Waters** (1835-70), kept a baby-farming establishment in this road before removing to Brixton. She was tried at the Old Bailey in September 1870 for the murder by poisoning of John Cowen aged 4 months. She was found guilty and hanged at Horsemonger Lane Gaol on 11th October 1870.

BRABOURN GROVE: The houses were built by George Avis of Hollydale Road between 1878 and 1879, and the street was taken over by the Vestry of Camberwell in 1879. William Jeremiah Goff (1829-1916), gardener, had an extensive nursery here. The site of the nursery and greenhouses was later used as a coach depot by Glenton Tours. There are plans currently afoot to redevelop the site for housing. Goff's daughter, Ethel, was the second wife of Ernest Brackley ((1882-1956), gatekeeper of Nunhead Cemetery. Ethel, who was related to Kate Carney, the famous music hall entertainer, died at Brabourn Grove in 1976.

BRACKLEY AVENUE, LINDEN GROVE: Built on the site of Linden Grove Estate 2002-3. Named after Ernest Brackley (1882-1956), who was gatekeeper at Nunhead Cemetery for 50 years. He lived at No 127 Linden Grove, almost opposite the cemetery gates, and is buried at Nunhead.

BRAYARDS ROAD: This street was laid out in the 1860s. The firm of Cooper and Kendall of Queen's Road, Peckham built around 55 houses here between 1877 and 1879. The street was taken over by the Vestry of Camberwell between 1869 and 1879. Originally known as Brayard Road, it was laid out on part of an ancient common arable field known at various times as Brayard, Bursted and the Braid. At one time it was known as Bursted Road. A part of Consort Road, where it adjoins Brayards Road, was shown on some street maps as 'The Braid' as late as 1890. Occupants in the early 1880s included: a solicitor, a music teacher, a mathematical instrument maker, a music publisher, a professor of billiards, and a shirt collar maker employing 25 females and a boy.

Corner of Brayards Road and Consort Road looking south in 1979.
The shop and the houses have since been demolished

BRENCHLEY GARDENS: This street leads from Brockley Way to Forest Hill Road. It was laid out in 1926 and commemorates William Brenchley (c.1858-1938), a former vestryman and councillor, who was Mayor of Camberwell 1911-12. He is buried in Camberwell New Cemetery, close to the street that bears his name. Council houses were built on part of the railway embankment following the closure of the railway line in 1954. Part of the embankment was incorporated into the park of the same name.

BROCK STREET: Originally a part of Tappesfield Road (q.v.). The name was suggested by the Nunhead Residents Association in 1979.

Charles Thomas Brock (1843-1881), pyrotechnist, was famous for organising grand firework displays at the Crystal Palace in Sydenham. In 1867 he was living at No 2 Beaufort Terrace, Nunhead Lane. In 1871 his address was Warwick House, Nunhead Lane, where he was residing with his wife Rhoda, and their adopted daughter, and two unmarried sisters. He employed two female servants and 42 'hands'. In 1874 the 'factory' at Kirkwood Road consisted of 30 wooden huts, and three brick buildings, spread over several fields reaching back to the railway embankment. Brock's head office was based at No 3, Percy Terrace, Nunhead Green. In 1875 he removed his business to Norwood.

BROCKLEY FOOTPATH: A public footpath sandwiched between the covered reservoirs of Thames Water and Nunhead Cemetery. It is all that remains of the ancient footpath that once led south from the Rye House Hotel at Peckham Rye to the Brockley Jack Tavern at Crofton Park.

Brockley Footpath in the 1970s. The boundary wall of Nunhead Cemetery is on the left. The covered reservoirs are on the right.

BROCKLEY WAY: A boundary road laid out in the 1930s between the former parishes of Camberwell and Lewisham. Originally a part of the ancient Brockley Footpath leading from Peckham Rye to the Brockley Jack Tavern and Brockley Hall at Crofton Park.

BROOKSTONE COURT, PECKHAM RYE: Built as a private block of flats on the east side of Peckham Rye between 1938 and 1940. It occupies the site of Beaufort House (q.v.). The first owners were Messrs Brook and Stone whom after whom the block is named. [Beasley].

BROWN'S GROUNDS, ST ASAPH ROAD: Sports grounds behind houses in Ivydale Road belonging to Haberdashers' Aske's Hatcham College. They were once known as Brown's Fields after William Brown, a tenant of the Haberdashers' Company. The Nunhead Football Club (q.v.) played here before and during the Second World War.

BUCHAN ROAD: Laid out c.1880 and taken over as a new street by the Vestry of Camberwell in 1888. According to W J A Hahn, former Chief Librarian of Camberwell Council, it may have been named after Andrew Buchan, Bishop of Caithness (1296). Most of the houses on the south side were demolished in the mid-1970s to make way for the Barset Estate.

Backs of houses in Buchan Road as seen from Linden Grove in 1972. The houses were demolished to make for the Barset Estate.

CAMBERWELL NEW CEMETERY, BRENCHLEY GARDENS: Now within the Forest Hill, London SE23 postal district. The land was acquired by the Borough of Camberwell in 1901. The central portion of the cemetery was purchased from Alfred Stevens of Homestall Farm, Peckham Rye in June 1901, for the sum of £11,305. The western section, adjoining One Tree Hill (about 32 acres) was bought from Alfred Stevens for close on £20,000. In November 1901, another plot adjoining Brockley

Footpath, comprising 12 acres was purchased from the Governor's of Christ's Hospital for £,6,325. The site, not immediately required for burial purposes, was let to the Honor Oak Golf Club, and a small plot was let to James Wells, pyrotechnist. The cemetery was laid out and consecrated by the Rt Revd William Woodcock Hough, Bishop of Woolwich, in 1927. It is now run by the London Borough of Southwark.

CAMBERWELL OLD CEMETERY, FOREST HILL ROAD: Now in the London SE22 (East Dulwich) postal district. The cemetery was opened by the Vestry of Camberwell in 1856 as 'The Burial Ground of Saint Giles's Parish in the County of Surrey, situate at Forest Hill, Peckham Rye, Surrey'. The cemetery layout and its buildings were designed by George (later Sir George) Gilbert Scott, who designed the new Church of St Giles at Camberwell. William Harnett Blanch (d.1900), the Camberwell historian, is buried here.

Gothic gate lodge in Camberwell Old Cemetery

CANDLE GROVE, LINDEN GROVE: Part of the new Linden Grove Estate built on the site of Linden House in 2002/3.

CARDEN ROAD: Laid out in the late 1860s and taken over by the Vestry of Camberwell in 1879. Occupants in 1881 included an architect, a civil engineer, an officer in the Royal Navy, and several civil servants. Possibly named after the parish of Carden in Cheshire [Sherwood].

Children posing for a photograph before being taken out for the day in 1947. The coach is parked in Carden Road outside St Antholin's Church.

CAULFIED ROAD: Originally a part of Lugard Road., and taken over as a new street by the Vestry of Camberwell in 1879. Renamed Caulfield Road in 1884, possibly after James Caulfield (1764-1826), author and print seller [Sherwood]. There was once a large factory at the corner of Caulfield and Brayards roads where Heinz and Company, famous for their baked beans and 57 varieties, produced pickles and sauces. The firm moved to north London in 1925.

CHABOT DRIVE, LINDEN GROVE: Built on the site of the Linden Grove Estate 2002-03. Named after the Chabots, an old Camberwell family, many of whom were in the medical profession. Edwin Chabot (1806-93), physician and surgeon, lived at No 4 Linden Grove until his death. He is buried in Nunhead Cemetery.

CHEAM STREET: A part of Banstead Street (q.v.) until 1979. The name was chosen to continue the Surrey connection. For example Nunhead was once in the County of Surrey and both streets cover the site of Surrey Lane, Surrey Square and Surrey Villas.

CHELTENHAM COLLEGE MISSION: A mission hall was built on a skittle alley behind the Belvedere Tavern (q.v.) in 1890. In 1932, the mission removed to the 'Swiss Chalet', now Westminster Youth Club, in Nunhead Grove. The old mission hall was afterwards used for commercial purposes and has since been demolished. The local scout troop was founded at the old mission by the Rev Edward Courtenay Dawson MA. With the outbreak of war in 1914, Father Dawson became a chaplain in the Royal Navy, and was on board the cruiser *HMS Majestic* when she was sunk. After the war he returned to Nunhead as a curate of St Antholin's and as Cheltenham College missioner, before becoming Archdeacon of Mauritius. In 1946 he was awarded the Bronze Cross for saving six Mauritian scouts from drowning. Father Dawson died in 1953 shortly after paying a return visit to his friends at Nunhead.

CHELTENHAM ROAD, NEWLANDS: Hall Road from 1901. Renamed Cheltenham Road July 1938. The section from Stuart Road to Hichisson Road was taken over as a new street by the Vestry of Camberwell in 1888, and the section from Hichisson Road to Ivydale Road was adopted in 1895. According to a former vicar of St Silas's Church the name commemorates Cheltenham College Mission which had premises in this road. The mission was based in Nunhead Grove (q.v.).
  William Nay Wilkins (1820-?) artist, lived at No 1 Swiss Villa, Hall Road. He was born in Dublin and was a surveyor and landscape painter. He exhibited at the Royal Academy and British Institute, and was the author of several works including, *What have they done with art since 1837* (1868). His wife, Lydia, who was long resident in Trinidad, recorded some of her impressions of the island in her book, *The Slave Son* (1853).
  Louis Gandolfi (1864-1932), camera maker, lived at No 84 Hall Road. He started his business in the Old Kent Road before moving into a disused hairpin factory in Borland Road, Newlands, in 1928.

CITRON TERRACE: A small housing development built by the Greater London Council c.1980 on the site of No 1 Linden Grove, a large Victorian house. The adjoining buildings are known as Basswood Close (q.v.). An association of names: citron, basswood and linden are trees.

CLAIRE COURT, PECKHAM RYE: This small block of flats on the western side of Peckham Rye overlooks the site of the Rye pond. It was built by the Tilt Estate Company of Peckham Rye in the 1980s. The name commemorates Claire, a granddaughter of Mrs Harvey (d.1976), a governing director of the Tilt Estate Company. [Beasley].

CLAUDE ROAD: Only a small section of this street, from Heaton Road to Godman Road, now exists. The Victorian houses have long since disappeared. The street was laid out on land originally owned by Sir Claude Champion de Crespigny, 4th baronet, of Champion Lodge, Camberwell, after whom it is named. The houses, several shops, and the handsome 'Claude Hotel', a splendid Victorian public house, were all demolished in the 1970s to make way for the Consort Housing Estate. The section from Scylla Road to Heaton Road, since redeveloped as part of the estate, was taken over by the Vestry of Camberwell as a new street in 1877. The section, from Heaton Road to Godman Road, was adopted in 1879.

CLOCK HOUSE, No 196a PECKHAM RYE: Built in 1883 as a dwelling house and offices for Roberts and Son, to the designs of Vincent John Grose FRIBA. It was later used as an off-licence. In 1962 it was taken over by Young and Co, brewers, who reopened it as a fully licensed public house in 1970.

COLYTON ROAD, PECKHAM RYE: This road leads from Forest Hill Road to Homestall Road. It was laid out in the 1880s and was known as Coliton Road until May 1911. It once bordered the grounds of Homestall Farm and several cricket fields, and was adopted by the Vestry of Camberwell between 1893 and 1898. The remaining section, from No 14 Colyton Road to Homestall Road, was adopted by Camberwell Borough Council in 1936.
 Percy Lane Oliver (1878-1944), a pioneer of the blood transfusion service, lived at No 5 (the house with the blue plaque). Before the Second World War he had created a blood transfusion network covering the whole of the UK. **Arthur Robinson Wright** ISO, FSA (1862-1932), civil servant, antiquarian and president of the Folklore Society, lived at No 8. He was editor of *Folklore*, and the author of many papers on anthropology. **Alderman John Somerville** (1842-1910), a former Mayor of Camberwell, lived at No 10. A later resident of No 10, **Edward Roberts** ISO, FRAS, JP (1845-1933), astronomer and mathematician, was chief assistant to the Nautical Almanac Office. **James Clements** (1876-1955) lived at No 32. He was Secretary of the London Cemetery Company, the founders of Nunhead and Highgate cemeteries, for 39 of the 65 years he spent in its service.

CONSORT ROAD: Originally a footway connecting Nunhead Lane to Peckham High Street. It was once known as Nunhead Road, and later as Albert Road, after the Prince Consort, from 1879 to 1938. It was taken over as a new street by the Vestry of Camberwell in 1869, and renamed Consort Road in July 1937. Many houses were demolished in the 1960s and 1970s.
 William Collier (1795-1871), journalist and music critic, lived at No 2 Augusta Place, Albert Road, demolished in 1990. He was editor and part owner of *The Court Gazette*, and the author of many plays including *The Blacksmith*, produced at the Coburg Theatre in 1834, and *The Rival Sergeants,* produced at Sadlers Wells in 1847. **Richard Radcliffe Pond** (1824-68), a lineal descendant of the Earl of Derwentwater, lived at No 1 Albert Villas, Albert Road. He was an advertising agent and a lessee of Drury Lane Theatre. **George Henry Heald** (1822-81), lecturer, lived and died at No 90 Albert Road. He was secretary of the Church of England Sunday School Institute 1855-72, and lecturer at Sunday schools 1872 to death. He was well-known to Sunday school teachers in all parts of the world. **Archibald Bruce Campbell** (1881-1966), broadcaster and author, was born at No 178 Albert Road. He found fame on BBC radio during the Second World War as one of the original members of *The Brains Trust*. In 1956 he had his own TV series *Calling on Campbell* in which he told his

seafaring tales; he was an officer in the navy during the war. He also wrote many books for both adults and children.

*COPELAND AVENUE, PECKHAM RYE: A small street off Copeland Road (q.v.) laid out in the 1880s. It disappeared when the Atwell Estate (q.v.) was built in the 1960s and is now covered by a car park.

Mabel Philipson *nee* **Russell** (1886-1951), actress and politician, was born at No 1 Copeland Avenue. She was a Gaiety Girl at the Gaiety Theatre and appeared in *The Merry Widow* in 1907. Turning her attention to politics, she succeeded her husband as MP for Berwick upon Tweed in 1923. She stood down from her seat in the general election of 1929, and resumed her acting career, retiring from the stage in 1933.

COPELAND ROAD, PECKHAM RYE: Originally called Cow Lane, a country lane connecting Peckham Rye with Cow Walk (now the north end of Consort Road) and High Street, Peckham. It was taken over by the Vestry of Camberwell in 1873, and renamed in 1875 after Copeland Terrace, one of several terraces in Cow Lane at that time. The origin of the name is uncertain. It may have been named after Chief Justice Copeland (d.1761), a supporter of Peckham's Hanover Chapel who is buried in Camberwell churchyard. The name Copeland Terrace was abolished in 1880, along with Caroline Terrace, John's Terrace, Royal Terrace and Woodbine Terrace. Most of the Victorian houses were demolished in the 1960s and 1970s and replaced by the Atwell Estate (q.v.). The road is now a busy by-pass for traffic.

George Humphrey Burke (1847-1920), professional cricketer, lived and died at No 28. A lower order right-handed batsman and right-arm fast bowler, he played in just one match for Kent County CC in 1877.

COSSALL ESTATE AND PARK: Built between 1977 and 1981. Several streets were demolished to create both the estate and the park including: Cossall Street, Mortlock Gardens, Hook's Road, Sunwell Street, Bidwell Street and parts of Harders, Gordon and Burchell roads.

CREWYS ROAD: The houses in this street were built by Cooper and Kendall between 1876 and 1879. The street was adopted by the Vestry of Camberwell in 1881. The first residents included an architect, a master builder, a master chemist and a master tailor. Several families employed a domestic servant.

Frederick Damer Cape (1829-82), journalist and songwriter, lived and died at No 24. He was the author of many songs in *Sharp's Vauxhall Comic Song Book* (1848-49), and wrote a song for the farewell benefit of the Ethiopian Serenaders performed at St James's Theatre in 1847.

CROSS CLOSE, GORDON ROAD: A small housing development built 1995 on the site of Nazareth House which was damaged by arsonists in 1991 and demolished in 1994. Nazareth House was built in 1857 for the Sisters of the Christian Retreat. The nuns left in 1865 when the construction of the railway adjoining their land took away their privacy. The vacated building was taken over by the Camberwell Guardians for a supplementary workhouse. In her novel, *The Ballad of Peckham Rye,* which is a mixture of fact and fiction, Muriel Spark writes of nuns being buried in the grounds of the convent but this is pure fantasy, as the nuns have a burial plot in Nunhead Cemetery.

*CROSS ROAD: A small stretch of road cutting across Peckham Rye Common connecting Nunhead Lane with East Dulwich Road. It became a part of East Dulwich Road in July 1937. The Peckham Rye Open Air Swimming Baths were here from 1923 until closed in 1987.

DANIEL'S ROAD: Laid out in the 1860s and adopted by the Vestry of Camberwell in 1885. The street was named after Henry Daniel (1805-67), monumental mason who was connected with Nunhead and Highgate cemeteries. His house, known as Church House, and masonry yards were situated at the end of the road. The houses were compulsorily purchased by the LCC in the late 1950s and demolished in 1960. Many people living in this street were descended from families who had lived in here since the 1860s. Sadly, an entire community was broken up in the name of progress.

Gladys Southwood pushing a pram in Daniel's Road c.1936

DENNETT'S ROAD: Built in the 1860s. Originally in the parish of Camberwell, it is listed under Peckham in the Post Office Directory 1867. It was transferred to the Borough of Deptford in 1902. Named after John Dennett (1790-1852), inventor of lifesaving rocket apparatus. (Read).

DR HAROLD MOODY PARK, CONSORT/GORDON ROADS: Originally a part of Consort open space created in the 1970s. It is named after Harold Arundel Moody (1882-1947), a famous West Indian doctor whose surgery was in Queen's Road, Peckham.

DUNDAS ROAD: Laid out in the early 1870s and adopted as a new street by the Vestry of Camberwell in 1876. The first occupants were mainly commercial clerks. Many houses were destroyed during the Second World War and were replaced by prefabricated bungalows known as prefabs. These have since been replaced by social housing.

EDINBURGH CASTLE, No 57 NUNHEAD LANE: A public house by this name has occupied this site since before 1862. It was rebuilt by its owners, Truman and Hanbury, brewers, in 1935, and was renamed 'Page Two' in 2003. It is now known as 'The Village Inn'.

ELLAND ROAD, NEWLANDS: In 1869, Thomas Drake (d.1877) of Oakfield Lodge, Peckham Rye, put forward proposals to build two new streets i.e. Elland Street and Siddall Street, on a site adjoining the land set aside by the Southwark and Vauxhall Water Company for their reservoirs. Siddall Street appears on a 1930 street map, but it doesn't appear to have been built. Elland Street was renamed Elland Road in August 1873, and was adopted by Camberwell Borough Council in 1908.

ELLERY STREET: George Street until October 1879. It was taken over as a new street by the Vestry of Camberwell in 1878, and may have been renamed in honour of Robert Ellery (1827-1908), astronomer of Australia, who was born in Surrey and visited England in 1875. [Sherwood]. In 1881 the occupants included a boot maker, a dairyman, a gardener, a law writer and a coach smith. The houses on the north side of the street were demolished in the 1970s to create Consort open space.

EVELINA ROAD: Originally a track and unnamed road connecting Nunhead Green with St Mary Magdalene's Church and St Mary's Road. The extreme eastern end, formerly in the parish of St Paul's Deptford, was known as Cemetery Road in 1869, and Lausanne Road until August 1881. The builder, Dadd, of Cemetery Road, started building here in 1871. The road was taken over as a new street by resolution of the Vestry of Camberwell in 1876. This is the main shopping street in Nunhead. J F Ayre's bakery was established at No 133 in 1955, on the site of Hiam's Bakery. F C Soper, fishmongers, was established 1897. Both shops attract customers from far and wide. The street may have been named after the novel 'Evelina' by Frances Burney (1752-1840). [Sherwood].
    Charles Peace (1832-79), Victorian burglar and murderer, lived at No 5 East Terrace, Evelina Road. Peace, accompanied by his 'wife' and a female servant, moved into the house in 1877. He gave is name as Thompson and appeared to be a perfectly respectable gentleman. Then one day in October 1878 he disappeared, never to be seen again. Puzzled residents later discovered that their quiet Mr Thompson was in fact the infamous villain Charles Peace who was hanged in 1879.

FERNHOLME ROAD, WAVERLEY PARK: Laid out as a new street in 1894 and adopted by the Vestry of Lewisham in 1898.

FIRBANK ROAD: Laid out in the 1870s, and taken over by the Vestry of Camberwell in 1879. The original tenants included a retired Royal Navy paymaster, a weaver of hearth rugs, and a forewoman in the baby linen trade. The street may have been owned by a Mr Firbank who paid the Vestry £10 towards the cost of paving repairs in 1870. [Sherwood].

FOREST HILL ROAD: Now in the London SE22 (East Dulwich) postal district. The street was once known as Wood Lane, Peckham Rye.
Boris Karloff (1887-1969), film actor, whose real name was William Pratt, was born in Forest Hill Road. He is best known for his role as Frankenstein's monster which he first played in 1931. **Liam MacCarthy** (1853-1928), lived and died at No 48a. A Camberwell Borough Councillor, he established the All-Ireland Hurling Games and set up the London League for Gaelic Football.

FORESTER ROAD: Originally called Forester Avenue, it was taken over as a new street by the Vestry of Camberwell in 1882, and renamed Forester Road in March 1888.

FRIERN ROAD SCHOOL, PECKHAM RYE: Opened as an elementary school by the London School Board in 1896. It became a secondary school for girls and was merged with Honor Oak Girls' School (q.v.) in 1978 to create Waverley School (q.v.), now Harris Academy.

*****GALATEA, No 208 CONSORT ROAD:** A Victorian public house which stood at the corner of Heaton and Consort roads. It was demolished in the 1970s to make way for Southwark Council's Consort Estate. Galatea is a sea nymph in Greek mythology.

*****GALATEA ROAD:** This street was laid out in the late 1860s on land owned by the de Crespignys of Camberwell. It was adopted by the Vestry of Camberwell in 1878. The street disappeared when the Consort Estate was built in the 1970s.

GALATEA SQUARE: Part of the huge Consort Estate built by Southwark Council in the 1970s. It perpetuates the name of Galatea Road.

GARDENS, THE, PECKHAM RYE: Formerly Layland Road, Maidlow Road and Newcombe Road. Large houses surround private gardens laid out for residents of the square in the late 1860s. Renamed 'The Gardens' in 1879 and adopted by Camberwell Borough Council in 1905. The houses were occupied by the well-heeled in the 1880s, and included a colonial broker, a civil engineer, a lawyer, a wine merchant, a retired consul, a retired army surgeon, and several stockbrokers.
William Michael Watson (c.1840-89), composer, who wrote under the name of Jules Favre, lived and died at No 28. A student of painting he

turned his attention to music in 1860, becoming a prolific songwriter. He founded the West End School of Music in 1883. His song *Anchored* was sold for over £1,200 in 1894. **Robert James Lees** (1849-1931), a Congregationalist and noted spiritualist, lived at No 26 in the 1890s. He founded the People's League which met at Central Hall, No 43 High Street, Peckham, and often addressed meetings of several thousand people.

GAUTREY ROAD: Edith Road from 1860 to 1937, it was taken over by the Vestry of Camberwell in 1876. Early occupants included a senior clerk at H M Dockyard, Deptford and an architect. It was renamed in July 1937 in honour of Thomas Gautrey (1852-1949), a former vestryman of Camberwell who was deputy chairman of the LCC.

GELLATLY ROAD: Situated across the border in the London Borough of Lewisham, it was once in the parish of Camberwell. The first residents gave their address as Nunhead (the street is near Nunhead Station). The road was laid out on land owned by the Haberdashers' Company and their property mark is attached to several corner houses. The street was placed in the London, SE14 (New Cross) postal district in 1917.
Harold Sydney Bride (1890-1956), assistant telegraphist on board the RMS *Titanic*, was born at No 31. He survived the sinking of the ill-fated White Star liner when on the 14th April 1912 it struck an iceberg and sank with the loss of over 1,500 lives of passengers and crew.

Gellatly Road 1904.

GIBBON ROAD: Originally a part of Cemetery Road, it was laid out in the 1840s to provide access from Queen's Road, Peckham to Nunhead Cemetery. A later name was Lausanne Road. It was renamed Gibbon Road in August 1881. L S Sherwood and J D Beasley, suggest it is named after Charles Gibbon, author and a former editor of the South London Press, while Joan Read, the Lewisham historian, suggests it commemorates Edward Gibbon, the historian, who lived at Lausanne in Switzerland. Part of the street, from Evelina Road to Linden Grove, was taken over by the Vestry of Camberwell in 1875. The section from Senate Street to Kitto Road was adopted in 1886. Realignment of the parish boundaries in 1900 placed the east side of the street in the newly created Metropolitan Borough Deptford, and since 1965 it has been in the London Borough of Lewisham. This was an important shopping street in the late 19th and early 20th century, and suffered much bomb damage during the Second World War. On the 15th June 1944 a VI flying bomb came down destroying the Alexander Hotel (q.v.) and several houses. Many houses in Senate Street (q.v.) and Gibbon Road were damaged beyond repair.

Willington Lodge, Gibbon Road, Nunhead, was built 1872, and was used for some time as offices by David C Preston & Co, monumental masons. It was demolished in 1975.

*GOLD DIGGERS ARMS, No 75 CONSORT ROAD: A Victorian pub at the corner of Brayards Road. It was badly damaged by arsonists in 1989, and was afterwards used as offices before being demolished in 2005. A housing development, completed 2007, now occupies the site.

Gold Diggers Arms after being damaged by fire in 1990.

GOLDEN ANCHOR, No 16 EVELINA ROAD: A public house with the same name has occupied this site since before 1880. It was rebuilt in the 20th century. The name has no local significance.

GODMAN ROAD: Donald Road until 1878 in which year it was adopted by the Vestry of Camberwell. It occupies land formerly owned by the de Crespigny family of Camberwell, and is said to be named after Major General Richard Temple Godman, husband of Eliza, eldest daughter of Sir Claude Champion de Crespigny. Occupants in 1881 included: an accountant, a fancy box maker, a policeman, a retired GPO clerk, a gardener, and two music teachers,

GORDON ROAD: Gordon Road first appears on street maps in the 1850s and is named on Stanford's map of 1862. The entire street, from Nunhead Green to Harders Road, Peckham, was adopted by the Vestry of Camberwell in 1869. It takes its name from Gordon Terrace, one of several terraces whose names were abolished in March 1875. It may have been named after General Gordon (1833-85) the hero of Khartoum. At the 1881 census the residents at the Nunhead Green end of Gordon Road included: several commercial clerks, a master engineer, a journalist, an ostrich feather merchant, a charcoal dealer and an artist in oil painting.

George Augustus Holmes (1861-1943), musician, was living with his parents at No 122 in 1881. He later removed to 'Auckland House' No 22 Linden Grove. **John Thomas Trunley** (1898-1944), known as 'The Peckham Fat Boy' moved to Gordon Road before the outbreak of the Second World War and opened a watch-menders shop at No 93 (since demolished). He found fame from a young age as the heaviest person in Britain and appeared on stage and in films. He toured with the 'Buffalo Bill Show' and was a friend of Charlie Chaplin.

Houses awaiting demolition in the 1980s. The site in Gordon Road is now covered by Habitat for Humanity houses.

GREENHIVE, BRAYARDS ROAD/CONSORT ROAD: A modern care home for the elderly built by Anchor Homes.

GRIMWADE CLOSE: A small housing development on the north side of Evelina Road completed in 1995. It covers the site of Grimwade Crescent (q.v.).

*GRIMWADE CRESCENT: Charles Grimwade, builder of No 2 Hollydale Road, built many houses in and around Nunhead in the 1870s and 1880s including Grimwade Crescent which bore his name. The street was adopted by the Vestry of Camberwell in 1878. The Victorian terraces were demolished in the 1970s as part of Southwark Council's Consort/ Barset redevelopment scheme. Part of the site was later used as an adventure playground for children, and the rest as allotment gardens until required for housing purposes. At the 1881 census the residents included: several labourers, an accountant, a certified teacher, a tram driver, a bootmaker, and someone who said he would do anything for a living. Grimwade Close (q.v.) was built on the site in 1995.

HABINTEG HOUSING DEVELOPMENT, NUNHEAD: Prime Minister Margaret Thatcher (now Lady Thatcher) opened the Habinteg housing development on 30th September 1980. The houses, which cover parts of Barset Road (q.v.), Tappesfield Street (q.v.) and Nunhead Grove (q.v.), were built to accommodate disabled people and their families.

HABITAT CLOSE, GORDON ROAD: Part of a 'Habitat for Humanity development'. The first stage of these self-built houses was completed in 1999. The Duke of Gloucester, the USA Ambassador, and the late Anita Roddick, founder of Body Shop, visited the building works in 1998. The new development occupies the site of several shops demolished in the 1980s, one of which was the former home of Johnny Trunley, 'The Peckham Fat Boy'.

HARLESCOTT ROAD, WAVERLEY PARK: This road was laid out between 1877 and 1884 and was adopted by Camberwell Borough Council in 1903. Harlescott is a place in Shropshire [Sherwood].

John Nisbet JP (1849-1925), land tax commissioner and councillor, lived at No 90 Harlescott Road. As secretary of 'The Enclosure of Honor Oak Protest Committee' he was instrumental in saving One Tree Hill Park (q.v.) for the people. He is buried in Camberwell Old Cemetery but his monument has been removed.

Harlescott Road 1930

HARRIS GIRLS' ACADEMY: Formerly Waverley Girls' School (q.v.) and Honor Oak Girls' School (q.v.). Named after Lord Harris of Peckham. The Academy opened in September 2006.

HATHORNE CLOSE, BRAYARDS ROAD: Built 1959-60. Named after a plot of land in Dulwich. [Sherwood/ Beasley].

HAWKSLADE ROAD, WAVERLEY PARK: Hawkslade Road was laid out in 1882 and by 1900 all the houses had been built. The street was adopted by Camberwell Borough Council in 1902. Possibly named after Hawk(e)slade, a place in Cumberland, or perhaps hawk and slade (valley) 'valley of the hawk'.

HAZEL CLOSE, see ATWELL ESTATE: Named after a hazel tree on the estate c.1963. [Beasley].

*HEADLEY STREET: Headley Street was a cul-de-sac on the western side of Gordon Road. It was adopted by the Vestry of Camberwell in 1879. Only seven houses were built and these were demolished in the late 1970s. The site is now covered by Consort Park.

*HEATON ARMS, No 249 RYE LANE: The Heaton Arms was built in the late 19th century and occupied the corner of Heaton Road opposite Rye Lane. Its address was No 1 Peckham Rye. Following the extension of Rye Lane in 1912, its address was changed to No 249 Rye Lane. For a brief period in the late 20th century it was known as the Duchess of Peckham and afterwards as the Vicar and Kilderkin, before reverting to its original name. It was demolished in 2005 and Co-operative House, a housing development, now covers the site.

HEATON ROAD, PECKHAM RYE: Partly laid out in the 1860s and extended in the 1870s. It was taken over by the Vestry of Camberwell in 1873, and gets its name from Isaac Heaton, brother-in-law of Sir Claude Champion de Crespigny, who built Heaton's Folly at Hanover Park, Peckham. The folly, a large church-like building, was constructed during a severe winter to give employment to 500 poor men in the neighbourhood. It was also known as 'The Paradise of Peckham'. In 1881 the residents of Heaton Road included: a lodging house keeper, a laundress, a chimney sweep, an actor, several stonemasons, a secretary to a building society, an accountant, and a merchant mariner.

HEATON ROAD CHURCH: This building has changed hands several times during the last hundred years. Opened in September 1873 as Zion Chapel by a group of Independents who previously met in a mission on Peckham Rye. The memorial stone was donated by David Cripps Preston (1842-1925), a vestryman and monumental mason of Gibbon Road, Nunhead.

HENLEY COURT, PECKHAM RYE: A small housing development built c.1990.

HICHISSON ROAD, NEWLANDS: Formerly Paddington Road. It was renamed in October 1891 and adopted by the Vestry of Camberwell in 1895. Named after Joseph Geldart Hichisson, a vestryman and later an alderman of Camberwell Borough Council.

HOLLYDALE ROAD: Laid out in the early 1870s and adopted by the Vestry of Camberwell in 1877. It stretches from Lugard Road, near Queen's Road, Peckham, to Nunhead Railway Station. Charles Grimwood, who built many houses in Nunhead, lived at No 2 Hollydale Road.

However, Cooper and Kendall of Queen's Road were responsible for building most of the houses in Hollydale Road. They began operations in 1876. Residents in 1881 included: a coal merchant and a retired civil servant. The name is probably an association of ideas, i.e. the holly and the ivy. Ivydale Road is close by. [Sherwood].

HOLLYDALE PRIMARY SCHOOL, HOLLYDALE ROAD: A school was first built on this site by the London School Board in 1877. The school was rebuilt in the 20th century.

HOLLYDALE TAVERN, No 115, HOLLYDALE ROAD: Built in the 1870s at the corner of Brayards and Hollydale roads. It is believed to have been the favourite pub of the infamous Victorian villain, Charles Peace (1832-79), who was hanged in 1879. He lived at No 5 East Terrace, Evelina Road, Nunhead.

HOMELEIGH ROAD, WAVERLEY PARK: This road was laid out in the 1880s. Homeleigh Road was in the parish of Lewisham before realignment of the parish boundaries in 1900. It was taken over as a new road by resolution of the Vestry of Lewisham in 1896.

HOMESTALL ROAD, PECKHAM RYE: This road runs alongside the former grounds of Homestall Farm, now Peckham Rye Park. It was an unmade road well into the 1950s and once led to Priory Farm, the last working farm in the area which existed until about 1914. Honor Oak Girls School (q.v.) was built in the grounds of Priory Farm in 1931, and the Aquarius Golf Club (q.v.) occupies another part of the site.

HONITON GARDENS, GIBBON ROAD: A low-rise housing development built by the LCC in 1959-60. Honiton is a place in Devon.

HONOR OAK CREMATORIUM, BROCKLEY WAY: Built by Camberwell Borough Council in 1938-39 on part of the land set aside for Camberwell New Cemetery. It was opened on 29th March 1939 by Lord Horder. By 1987 over 97,500 bodies had been cremated here. Since 1965 it has been run by Southwark Council.

HONOR OAK GIRLS' SCHOOL, HOMESTALL ROAD: The first open-air type secondary school to be built by the London County Council.

It was built from the designs of G Topham Forest FRIBA, and opened by the president of the Board of Education, the Rt Hon H B Lees-Smith on the 21st May 1931. Miss A M Ashley MA was the first headmistress and retired in 1951. The school merged with Friern Secondary Modern Girls' School in 1978 and became Waverley Comprehensive Girls' School (q.v.). Many new buildings have been erected in the grounds and the school is now known as the Harris Academy.

Honor Oak Girl's School in 1973

HOWBURY ROAD: Laid out c.1877 and adopted by the Vestry of Camberwell in 1886. Howbury is a place near Slade Green in Kent. The first occupants included several firework makers, a gravedigger, two carpenters, and the Revd James Field, a 74-year-old Church of England clergyman who was without the care of souls.
William John Fairservice (1881-1971), cricketer, was living at No 34 in 1891. He removed to Tonbridge in Kent and joined Kent CCC in 1902. He retired from professional cricket in 1921 having played in 302 first-class matches. **Doug Baker** (1921-2005), shoemaker and artist, was living at No 17 at the time of his death. A clicker by trade, he spent 51 years with H & M Rayne Ltd, cutting out leather for shoes. His customers included stars of stage and screen. He took up drawing in retirement and published some of his sketches in *Drawing a Line from Here and There* (1988).

HUGUENOT SQUARE, PECKHAM RYE: Part of Southwark Council's huge Consort housing development which was completed in 1978. The name perpetuates Huguenot Road (q.v.), one of several streets bulldozed to make way for the housing estate.

*HUGUENOT ROAD: Laid out in the 1870s on land owned by the de Crespigny family of Camberwell. It was known as Cadenham Road until June 1878, and was adopted by the Vestry of Camberwell in 1886. It disappeared when the Consort Estate was built in the 1970s. The de Crespigny's were Huguenots. Residents in 1881 were general labourers and commercial clerks although several houses were unoccupied.

INVERTON ROAD: This street borders the Waverley Park Estate. It was laid out in the early 1880s and taken over as a new street by Camberwell Borough Council in 1900. It may have been named after a place in Scotland. [Beasley].

    Geoffrey James Whittaker *aka* **Jimmy Whittaker (1916-97)** professional cricketer, was born at No 2a Inverton Road. An 'aggressive' middle order right-handed batsman, he played in 124 matches for Surrey CCC between 1937 and 1953, hitting 1,000 runs in 1949 and completing 1,439 runs in 1951. In his first-class career he played in 129 matches and scored 4,988 runs at an average of 29.16. The highest of his eight centuries was 185 not out. He also played as an amateur for Nunhead Football Club (q.v.) from 1934 to 1939 and perfected the sliding tackle.

IRIS COURT, BRAYARDS ROAD: Built on the site of Austin's antique shop, Nos 39-41 Brayards Road which closed in 1990. George Austin (1845-1927), an Oxfordshire man, opened the 'Oxford Farm Dairy' here in 1864. As well as supplying milk, he became a contractor for removals 'in connection with the entire system of railways'. In 1923 he claimed to be the oldest furniture remover in south London. He later became a second-hand furniture dealer and opened a large store at Peckham Rye. *See Austin Court.*

IVYDALE ROAD, WAVERLEY PARK: Ivydale Road was laid out by Edward Yates (1838-1907) between 1877 and 1884. The section from Gibbon Road to Limesford Road (south of the cemetery) was taken over by the Vestry of Camberwell as a new street in 1887, and the section from Limesford Road to the old parish boundary was taken over in 1890. The name may have been chosen because the road lies in a dale between hilly

Nunhead Cemetery and Telegraph Hill, and ivy was much planted in Victorian cemeteries. On the 12th August 1944, a VI flying bomb came down near St Silas's Church (q.v.) destroying 10 houses and killing two people. A few days later another came down in the same street and killed another three people.

Revd Thomas George John Crippen (1841-1929), Congregational historian and hymnologist, lived at No 270 (destroyed in the Second World War). He was librarian to the Congregational Library from 1896 to 1925, and contributed articles to the *Victoria County History*. He published several volumes of history and biography and wrote many hymns.

IVYDALE ROAD SCHOOL, WAVERLEY PARK: In 1888 a temporary school was built here by the London School Board. It was replaced by the present three-storey building in 1893. Thomas Henry Cotton (1907-87), golfer, better known as Sir Henry Cotton, attended the school with his brother Leslie.

*JAMES PLACE, NUNHEAD LANE: A terrace adjoining the Edinburgh Castle (q.v.) demolished in the 1960s for the New James Court Housing Estate (q.v.).

Mutton Davis (1795-1867) lived here. A colourful character, he gained his nickname for his insatiable appetite for mutton, and was well known throughout the parish of Camberwell as a boxer, wrestler and acrobat. A tailor by trade, one of his more unusual acrobatic feats was to amuse his customers by balancing a glass of ale on the ball of his foot, and raising the glass to his mouth and drinking the lot without spilling a drop!

KELVINGTON ROAD: Originally an unnamed road and footpath connecting the Newlands area to One Tree Hill at Honor Oak. The Kelvington Road Council Estate was built by Camberwell Borough Council in 1922, and the street was adopted by the council in the same year. The road was extended to Brenchley Gardens when the railway line closed and the bridge over the public footpath was removed in 1954.

KIMBERLEY AVENUE: Kimberley Road from 1867 to 1937. It was adopted by the Vestry of Camberwell in 1878. In 1881 the occupants included a journalist, a horse keeper, a railway signalman, a coach builder, a police constable, a shipwright, and a post-office overseer. Several houses were uninhabited. On the 30th June 1944 a VI flying bomb came down at the corner of Kimberley Avenue and Evelina Road (q.v.) killing three people. Many houses were destroyed including the former residence of Charles Peace, the Victorian murderer, who was hanged in 1879. Possibly named after John Wodehouse, statesman (d.1902), who was created Earl Kimberley in 1866 [Sherwood].

William John Fairservice (1881-1971), cricketer, was born at No 26, and was lodging with a postman at No 34 Howbury Road in 1901. His occupation was storekeeper and 'part time games player'. He joined his grandfather at Tonbridge and attended the Tonbridge 'Cricket' Nursery under the guidance of Captain William McCanlis (1840-1925), joining Kent CCC in 1902. He retired from first-class cricket in 1921, having played in 302 matches, making 4,939 runs in 419 innings and holding 164 catches. As a medium pace off-break bowler he had 859 wickets to his credit.

KINGDOM HALL (JEHOVAH'S WITNESSES), SCYLLA ROAD: Built in 1993 on the site of Scylla Hall (Plymouth Brethren).

KING'S ARMS, No 132 PECKHAM RYE: Renamed 'King's on the Rye' before being converted to a block of flats in 2000. The present building dates from 1957 and covers the site of the an earlier pub destroyed by a landmine in the Second World War. In 1835 Prince's 'Duke of Richmond' omnibus operated from here to the City. His stables were located behind the pub. The stables were later taken over by Thomas Tilling. In the 1920s the 'King's Arms' was well-known for its orchestral concerts and 'sumptuously-appointed tea-room and gardens.'

The old King's Arms in 1903. Warwick Place is on the right.

KIRKWOOD ROAD: Kirkwood Road follows the line of a country lane which was known as Hooks Lane and later as Slough Lane. The section from Nunhead Green to Bra yards Road was adopted as a new street by the Vestry of Camberwell in 1874. The remaining section from Bra yards Road to the modern Costal Estate was taken over in 1878. Possibly named after a place in Dumfriesshire [Sherwood]. Some of the first residents included a genealogist, a scripture reader, an optician, a messenger at the British Museum and a GPO (post office) clerk.

Ernest Theodore Corben (1885-1912), crew member on board the ill-fated RMS *Titanic*, lived at No 163. He is believed to have drowned when the liner struck an iceberg in April 1912. His body was never recovered.

KITTO ROAD: Laid out in the 1870s. The west end was in the parish of Camberwell and was adopted by the Vestry of Camberwell in 1889. The remainder was once in the parish of St Paul's Deptford, later Borough of Deptford, and since 1965 it has been in the London Borough of Lewisham. It may be named after the Revd Dr John Kato (1804-54), a missionary and religious author. (Read).

LANBURY ROAD, WAVERLEY PARK: Although it was laid out between 1877 and 1884, this street wasn't adopted by Camberwell Borough Council until 1922. The origin of the name is unknown.

LANVANOR ROAD: Taken over by the Vestry of Camberwell in 1879. Occupants in 1881 included: a shorthand writer, a publisher and a commercial traveller. The origin of the name is unknown.

LAUSANNE ROAD: Laid out in 1840 as the approach road from Peckham to Nunhead Cemetery. It was known as Cemetery Road until 1869 and took its name from Lausanne Villas, one of a group of houses in the road. Adopted by the Vestry of Camberwell in 1874. The east side was once in the Metropolitan Borough of Deptford and is now in the London Borough of Lewisham. Occupants in 1881 included a yeast merchant, a silk merchant, a property owner, a stockbroker, two master mariners, and a wholesale clothier who employed 470 workers.

John Pateshall Allen JP (1827-1904), domestic sewing machine manufacturer, lived and died at No 91. **Sgt-Major Joseph Harris** (1827-1902), Yeoman of the Guard (Beefeater) at the Tower of London, lived and died at No 76. As Quarter-Master Sergeant Harris of the 84th Regiment, he saw service in the Crimean Campaign and Indian Mutiny.

LIMES WALK: A small housing development in Linden Grove, including sheltered housing, dating from 1966-70. Built for Southwark Council on the site of the house and grounds of the Friary of the Brotherhood of the Holy Cross to the designs of Nylon and Unless.

LIMESFORD ROAD, WAVERLEY PARK: Laid out between 1877 and 1884. Lime is another name for the Linden tree. Linden Grove borders the northern side of Nunhead Cemetery and Limes ford Road borders the southern side. It was adopted by the Vestry of Camberwell in 1890. The completion of the Waverley Park Estate encouraged the London Cemetery Company to create a new entrance to Nunhead Cemetery in Limes ford Road which was built in 1909.
    Harry Quench (1858-1913), socialist and trade unionist, lived at No 35. He was one of the original members of the Democratic Federation, which included among its recruits, Eleanor, the daughter of Karl Marx. He was for many years the editor of the Federation's journal *Justice*.

LINDEN GROVE: Formerly Cemetery Road. The section from Daniel's Road to Gibbon Road was also known as Lausanne Road for a time. Laid out in 1840 connecting Nunhead Lane with Nunhead Cemetery. A grove of lime (linden) trees was planted from Nunhead Lane to the cemetery gates and continued into the cemetery. The limes along Linden Grove were felled in the 1950s. Linden Grove was taken over as a new street by the Vestry of Camberwell between 1882 and 1892. At the time of the 1881 census its residents included a civil engineer, an accountant, and a master watch maker. Many families employed domestic servants.
    Revd Canon George Potter (1887-1960), lived at 'The Friary', now covered by Limes Walk (q.v.). He founded the Brotherhood of the Holy Cross in 1924, and cared for hundreds of delinquent boys over the years. He was the author of two autobiographical books, *Father Potter of Peckham* (1955) and *More Father Potter of Peckham* (1958). **Alfred Monte Smith** (1828-1891), chorister, lived and died at No 7. A Gentleman of HM Chapels Royal and professor of singing at the Royal Academy of Music, he also composed many prize-winning glees and played Damon in Handel's *Aces and Galatea* at the Princess Theatre in 1869. **Ellen Tern an** (1839-1914), actress, lived at No 31 'Windsor Lodge'. She was Charles Dickens's mistress and he provided her with the 'secret' house at Nunhead and was a frequent visitor there. **Revd Isaac Haycroft** (1830-93), former chaplain to Lord Strafford, and vicar of St Chrysostom's, Peckham, lived at No 39. He was Anglican chaplain at Nunhead Cemetery in 1880. **Augustus Holmes** (1861-1943), organist and composer, lived at No 22

'Auckland House'. He was the author of preparatory manuals for piano and violin, and was Director of Examinations at the London College of Music. **Nicholas Gibbs Wanostrocht** (1833-95), schoolmaster, lived at Albion Villas. He was the son of Nicholas 'Felix' Wanostrocht, a famous cricketer. **William Henry Phillips** (1808-84), civil engineer, lived and died at No 119 'Church House'. He was the inventor of 'Phillips Fire Annihilator' patented in 1844, and wrote 'On aerial locomotion by machinery without gaseous buoyancy'. **Samuel Hulme Day** known as **Sammy Day** (1878-1950), professional cricketer, was born at No 7. He was the son of Sydney Townsend Day, wine merchant. His grandfather was Samuel Hulme Day JP, DL, of Beaufort House, Peckham Rye (q.v.). His family removed to Blackheath when Samuel was just three-years-old. He played in 128 matches for Kent CCC between 1897 and 1919, scoring a total of 5,893 runs.

Linden Grove c.1904

*LINDEN TAVERN, LINDEN GROVE: Built at the corner of Linden Grove and Nunhead Grove opposite the Belvedere Tavern (q.v.). It became a coffee tavern and was demolished in the 1930s.

LINDO STREET: A cul-de-sac, originally shared between the parishes of St Giles, Camberwell and St Paul's, Deptford. It was laid out in the 1860s and adopted by the Vestry of Camberwell in 1889. Occupants in 1881 were mostly general labourers. It may have been named after Elias Haim Lindo (1783-1857), an Anglo-Jewish historian. [Sherwood].

*LLOYD'S HEAD, PECKHAM RYE: This pub was near the White Horse Tavern (q.v.) and appears on maps in the 1860s and as late as 1890.

*LONDON, CAMBERWELL & DULWICH TRAMWAY CO: This company operated a single line horse-drawn tram service from Hollydale Road to the Dulwich Plough, via Brayards Road (q.v.), Copeland Road (q.v.) and Atwell Street (q.v.), with a branch line to the Triangle (Heaton Arms) at Peckham Rye. The tram service wasn't successful, operating for just five years between 1896 and 1901. The London County Council took over the company in 1904 and lifted most of the tracks in 1906.

LUGARD ROAD: Laid out in the 1870s, and known as Gurdon Road to May 1877 and Hollydale Road (part) to April 1938. Taken over by the Vestry of Camberwell between 1877 and 1879. At the time of the 1881 census its residents included a tram driver, several shop assistants, and a Chelsea Pensioner. It may have been named after General Sir Edward Lugard (1810-98), soldier and politician, who became Under Secretary, War Department. [Sherwood and Beasley].

    Alan Leo, formerly **William Frederick Allen** (1860-1917), astrologer, moved to No 12 Lugard Road in 1888 where he remained for about 10 years before removing to Hampstead. In 1889, together with another astrologer, he began his first monthly publication, *The Astrologers Magazine,* this was followed in 1895 by *Modern Astrology.* He was the author of several books on astrology.

*LUGARD TAVERN, LUGARD ROAD: This pub stood at the corner of Lugard and Stanbury roads and was destroyed during the Second World War.

LULWORTH ROAD: The houses in this street were built by Cooper and Kendall of Queen's Road, Peckham in 1878-79. The road was taken over by the Vestry of Camberwell in 1881. The first occupants were mostly commercial clerks.

MACHELL ROAD: J Dadd of Cemetery Road built all the houses in this road between 1878 and 1879. It was adopted by the Vestry of Camberwell in 1888. The first occupants included: a printer, a retired schoolmaster and a stonemason. At the time of the 1881 census several houses were unoccupied. Possibly named after James Octavius Machell (d.1902), a racehorse owner. [Sherwood].

MAGDALENE CLOSE: A small housing development at the corner of Heaton and Consort roads built by Southwark Council in the late 1970s and early 1980s. It was so-named due to its proximity to St Mary Magdalene School.

MAN OF KENT, Nos 2-4 NUNHEAD GREEN: This pub was originally built in the 1870s, and rebuilt between the two World Wars. The name was probably chosen because Nunhead was close to the Kent/Surrey border. In early documents Nunhead is sometimes described as being situated in Kent.

MANATON CLOSE. CONSORT ESTATE: Laid out in 1979-80 near the site of Manaton Road. *See next*.

***MANATON ROAD:** Laid out in the 1870s on land owned by the de Crespigny family of Camberwell, and taken over by the Vestry of Camberwell in 1877. The street disappeared when the Consort Estate was built in the late 1970s. The first occupants included three stone masons, a musician, a draughtsman, and a comedian (actor). Manaton is a place in Devon.

MAYA CLOSE, GORDON ROAD: A small housing development built in the late 1990s on the site of a builder's yard.

***MAY'S PLACE:** Known as May Place in the 19th century, part of the hamlet of Nunhead. The original cottages were built in the 18th century on the site of a bowling alley alongside the Old Nun's Head Tavern. They were pulled down in the 1870s and replaced by 12 houses known as Nunhead Cottages and Nun's Head Cottages. These were demolished in the 1970s to make way for Monteagle Way Council Estate (q.v.). Occupants in 1881 included: a journeyman baker, a number of general labourers, a laundress, and a gardener.

May's Place (houses on the right) 1974

MERTTINS ROAD, WAVERLEY PARK: Originally part of Brockley Footpath. Laid out by Edward Yates in 1884 and taken over by the Vestry of Lewisham in 1896. It was transferred to the newly created Metropolitan Borough of Camberwell in 1900, and is now in the London Borough of Southwark. The origin of the name is not known.
   Cecil Aubrey Gwynne Manning DL, JP (c.1893-1985), a former Mayor of Camberwell, lived No 2. He served on the council from 1931 to 1954, and organised the Borough of Camberwell's Golden Jubilee in 1950. He was MP (Labour) for North Camberwell from 1944 to 1950.

MONTEAGLE WAY: Built in 1979 as part of Southwark Council's Consort/Barset Development Scheme. It covers the site of May's Place (q.v.) and some shops and houses fronting Consort Road. It is named after Lord Monteagle (1790-1866) patron of the Metropolitan Beer and Wine Society, who laid the foundation stone of the Society's homes at Nunhead Green in 1852.

MORNING STAR, Nos 231/235 RYE LANE, PECKHAM RYE: This pub has been renamed 'The Nag's Head' following the success of BBC TV's series 'Only Fools and Horses' which was based in Peckham. The original pub was built at 'The Triangle', at the corner of Heaton Road and Peckham Rye in the late 19th century and was rebuilt in the 20th century.

The Big House from a painting by the author

NAZARETH GARDENS, GORDON ROAD: Built on the site of the Camberwell Reception Centre. Known locally as 'The Big House' or

'The Spike', it was for many years a refuge for homeless men. It was built in 1878 as the Camberwell Parish Workhouse in the grounds of a convent known as 'Nazareth House'. The reception area in front of the main building was added in 1879 and demolished in 1995 along with the chapel. The former workhouse was converted into 20 flats in the late 1990s.

NAZARETH HOUSE: *See Cross Close and Nazareth Gardens.*

NEW JAMES COURT: Part of a low-rise council housing development built in the 1960s by the LCC/GLC on the site of New James Street (q.v.). A row of shops and several large houses in Nunhead Lane and Scylla Road were demolished to make way for this development.

*NEW JAMES STREET: Originally a passage for pedestrians. Lined with houses on both sides, it led from Nunhead Lane to Scylla Road. It was adopted by the Vestry of Camberwell in 1896. The houses were demolished in the 1950s to make way for New James Court Estate (q.v.).

NEWLANDS: An area to the south of Nunhead and Peckham Rye. It was the last part of the ancient parish of Camberwell to be built on between 1870 and 1900. Joseph Dickason, dairy farmer, who ran the Newlands Dairy Farm, was a vestryman in the 1890s and a member of the General Purposes Committee 1893-4.

NEWLANDS TAVERN, No 40 STUART ROAD: Built before 1880 and rebuilt between the two World Wars. It was named after the district in which it was built, and was run by Thomas Dickason, beerseller. It was a popular rock venue in the late 1960s and early 1970s. Jeff Beck, Dr Feelgood and the Kursaal Flyers performed here, and the late Ian Dury made his first South London appearance here with his band the Kilburn High Roads. The pub was renamed the Stuart Arms in 1980s and is now the Ivy House.

NIGEL ROAD, PECKHAM RYE: Adopted by the Vestry of Camberwell in 1877. At the time of the 1881 census the residents included an oyster merchant, a City of London bailiff, a telegraph superintendent, a dentist, a municipal sanitary inspector, and several commercial clerks. Only three of the householders were born in the parish of Camberwell.
    William Margrie (1878-1960), founder of the London Explorers Club in

1930, lived and died at 'Sage Cottage' No 24. Self-styled the 'Sage of Camberwell' he wrote several books including *Rosemary Street* (1923), *Maggots and Men* (1924), and *Historical Camberwell* (1933). He also edited *The Pickwicks of Peckham* (1938).

NUNHEAD BAPTIST CHURCH, GAUTREY ROAD: In 1868 a Baptist church was started in Lausanne Road (q.v.) by the Revd Thomas Cole (1822-1902), who was Nonconformist chaplain at Nunhead Cemetery (q.v.) for 30 years. The congregation removed to a new chapel in Edith Road (now Gautrey Road) in 1888. The new chapel was built to the designs of G C Searle and Sons. After the Second World War the chapel was used for commercial purposes until 1991, when it was acquired by the Emmanuel Miracle Temple of Bethany Fellowship.

Nunhead Bus Garage 1952

*NUNHEAD BUS GARAGE, Nos 20-26 NUNHEAD LANE: Erected in 1911 to stable the fleet of Clarkson steam buses operated by the National Steam Car Company. In 1919 the company ceased operations and the garage was taken over by the London General Omnibus Company. In 1933 it was acquired by the London Passenger Transport Board, later London Transport. The garage was closed as an operational unit in February 1954 and was used for the maintenance of vehicles. In 1958 Charles William Banfield (d.1966) who had worked at Nunhead Lane as a driver for the LGOC, acquired the garage for his fleet of luxury coaches. He founded his coach business in 1928 with just one vehicle which he bought for £40. At the time of his death the company operated over 200 vehicles. His son Michael, took over the running of the business which was sold in

1973. The disused garage was afterwards used as a warehouse. It was demolished in 1999 and new housing now occupies the site. *See* Banfield Road.

NUNHEAD CEMETERY: The Cemetery of All Saints, Nunhead, was laid out by the London Cemetery Company in 1839-40, and the larger part of the 52-acre site was consecrated by the Bishop of Winchester in July 1840. The architect was James Bunstone Bunning (1802-63). Two chapels were built in 1844. In 1975, following several years of neglect, the cemetery was compulsorily purchased by Southwark Council. It was partially restored with lottery money in 2000 and is now a Grade II* listed landscape. The Friends of Nunhead Cemetery (founded 1981) manage the cemetery together with Southwark Council.

Main entrance to Nunhead Cemetery in Linden Grove 1972

NUNHEAD CHRISTIAN BAND, NUNHEAD GROVE: A mission hall built in 1901 for the Friends of Peckham Rye and the Free Salvationists, a breakaway group of the Salvation Army. The Revd W Wray was the architect, and foundation stones were laid by Matthew Wallace (1848-1917), the first mayor of the Borough of Camberwell, and Charles Goddard Clarke (1849-1908), Peckham's last Liberal MP. The building was taken over by Southwark Council in 1978 for use as a day centre for senior citizens. It is currently out of use and its future is uncertain.

NUNHEAD CRESCENT, PECKHAM RYE: Formerly Rye Crescent, a thoroughfare connecting Peckham Rye with Nunhead Lane. It was taken over by the Vestry of Camberwell in 1870. The houses and shops were demolished in the 1950s to make way for the Nunhead Estate (q.v.). The name is still in use within the estate.

NUNHEAD ESTATE: Five blocks of flats either side of Nunhead Lane and adjoining Peckham Rye. They were built by the London County Council between 1947 and 1959 on the site of Thomson's Corset Factory and Oregon and Beaufort Terraces, all destroyed by a flying bomb in 1944, and the site of the old Nunhead Crescent (q.v.). The blocks were named after omnibus and coach proprietors due to the proximity of Nunhead Bus Garage (q.v.). They are: Tilling House 1947; Lancefield House 1950; Glover House 1951; Goodwin House 1956, and Creed House 1959.

Nunhead FC 1936. John Lockton is standing at the back on the far right.

*NUNHEAD FOOTBALL CLUB: Nunhead FC was founded in 1888 and wound up in 1949. Several great footballers, including Leslie Henley, who went on to play for Arsenal and Reading, played for Nunhead in 1939-40. Others of note were John Henry Lockton (1892-1972) who played inside left as an amateur for both Nunhead and Crystal Palace. He also played first-class cricket for Surrey and received his county cap in

1920. Denis Compton (1918-97), the great cricketer and footballer, played as a left winger for Nunhead and signed for Arsenal in 1935. Reg Lewis (d.1997), another Arsenal player, gained his experience at Nunhead. His two goals in the 1950 Cup Final against Liverpool won the FA Cup for Arsenal. Sadly, Nunhead FC was forced to close when their benefactor's timber firm was destroyed in the Blitz. The club was finally wound up in 1949. *See* Brown's Grounds.

*NUNHEAD GRAMMAR SCHOOL: Manor House, a building which until recently stood at the corner of Nunhead Green and Gordon Road, was once a grammar school for boys. In 1867 it was run by John George Thompson. In 1881 it was run by James Lewis BA of Trinity College, Dublin. By 1901 the house was occupied by Robert Davey, a builder. It changed hands several times during the next 100 years and was a perfumery for a time. Its last occupant was an antique furniture restorer who moved out in 2004. The house was demolished in 2006.

NUNHEAD GREEN: Once known as Nun Green. The Vestry of Camberwell acquired the site from the Lord of the Manor in 1868, on condition that it remained open to the public in perpetuity. It was partially paved over with tarmac in the late 19th century and returned to a grassed area in the 1980s.

Nunhead Green c.1903

NUNHEAD GREEN BAPTIST CHAPEL: This chapel was situated between the Old Nun's Head pub (q.v.) and Manor House. It had 250 seats and a Sunday School at the rear. The building, together with Manor House, was occupied by Peter Allen Antiques until 2004. Both buildings were demolished in the summer of 2006. At the time of writing flats and commercial units are being built on the site.

Victorian cottages in Nunhead Grove 1972

NUNHEAD GROVE: One of Nunhead's oldest streets. It follows the line of the ancient Brockley Footpath and was adopted by the Vestry of Camberwell in 1865. At the time of the 1881 census, Nos 1, 2 and 3 Florence Villas (Florence Terrace) were still being built. The names of all the terraces, including Florence Terrace, Nunhead Terrace, Montague Villas, and Daniel's Cottages, were abolished when the street was renumbered in 1889. At the time of the 1881 census the residents included: a boot and shoe maker, a grocer, and a shoemaker. The architect and civil engineer, Robert Philip Pope, lived at No 2 Montague Villas, Nunhead Grove. A Victorian terrace on the east side was demolished in the 1960s to make way for the Tappesfield Estate completed in 1966. Several more houses were demolished in the 1970s. In October 1903, a shocking event took place in this quiet street. Sagatel Sagouni (c.1866-1903), President of the Armenian Revolutionary Society, was returning to his lodgings at No 29 Nunhead Grove, after attending a meeting of a secret society known as the Anglo-Armenian Club, when he was approached by a man who shot him dead at point blank range. His assassin, Yorgie Yannie, a fellow countryman from a breakaway group of the Armenian Revolutionary Party, killed two more members at Peckham Rye, before shooting himself. Sagouni was a millionaire having made his money in oil production in Russia. According to newspaper reports he was a peaceable and charitable man and built an Armenian church in Paris.

John Tanswell (1800-64) a lawyer and distinguished antiquarian lived at Temple House, Nunhead Grove. He was the author of *The History and Antiquities of Lambeth* (1858). After his death the property passed to his nephew **Thomas Pitts Taswell-Langmead BA, BCL** (1840-82), a barrister and professor of constitutional law at University College, London, and the author of several works including *Parish Registers - A plea for their preservation* (1872).

NUNHEAD LANE: Modern Nunhead Lane follows the line of an ancient country lane connecting the hamlet of Peckham Rye with the hamlet of Nunhead. By 1841 only a few houses had been built, one of which was a boarding school for young ladies between the ages of 10 and 15. Another house was occupied by Jesse Goody (1791-1843), a commercial clerk and his family. He was one of the first to be interred in the shaft catacomb in the Dissenters' section at Nunhead Cemetery. Most of the terraces were built in the 1860s and 1870s.

Nunhead Lane 1972

John Dickson (1790-1880), Waterloo veteran, lived and died at No 6 Philbrick Terrace (renumbered as part of Nunhead Lane in 1889). He rode with the Royal Scots Greys at the Battle of Waterloo and was promoted to troop sergeant-major. **David Orme** (1948 -), children's author, lived above a shop next door to St Antony's Church (q.v.) between 1960 and 1962, before removing to East Dulwich. He was a teacher for 18 years before becoming a full time writer. He has written over 250 books including poetry collections, fiction and non-fiction, and school text books.

Shops in Nunhead Lane being demolished in 1974

NUNHEAD LIBRARY: The library was built in the grounds of the Red Pottery Works in 1896. It was designed by Robert Phillipps Whellock (1834-1905) and was given to the people of Camberwell by the philanthropist John Passmore Edwards.

NUNHEAD PASSAGE: An ancient footway leading from Peckham Rye Common to the Old Nun's Head Tavern. All that remains is 72 yards from Peckham Rye to Whorlton Road. Scylla Road was once part of the old footpath.

NUNHEAD RAILWAY STATION, GIBBON ROAD: The present station dates from 1925 in which year the line was electrified. The original station, known as Nunhead Junction, was located on the other side of the road, and was built in 1871. During the construction of the railway the owners of Nunhead Cemetery complained that the railway works obstructed the approach road to the cemetery and prevented funerals taking place. Under the railway bridge, and set into a wall, is a Victorian post box. The booking office (pictured overleaf) dated from the 1920s and was demolished in 1999.

NUNHEAD RESERVOIRS, LINDEN GROVE: Four covered reservoirs were built on Nunhead Hill by the Southwark and Vauxhall Water Company between 1871 and 1875 on land acquired in 1854. John Aird

Nunhead Station and booking office in 1974

(1800-76) a great Victorian public contractor, constructed the mains and pumps. He is buried at Nunhead. The reservoirs were taken over by the Metropolitan Water Board in 1904. The four brick-built reservoirs were demolished by Thames Water and replaced by two concrete ones in 1994.

NUNHEAD RESIDENTS ASSOCIATION: Founded in 1973 following a meeting of concerned residents who were worried about Southwark Council's proposals to redevelop Nunhead. The first chairman was the Revd Andrew Grant of St Antony's Church (q.v.). The NRA was based at No 100 Evelina Road from 1973 to 1983. Meetings are now held in Nunhead Library.

OAKDALE ROAD: Formerly a part of Ivydale Road leading from Nunhead Railway Station (q.v.) to the junction of St Asaph Road (q.v.) and Linden Grove (q.v.). Renamed in 1980 in keeping with its former name.

OLD JAMES STREET: Taken over as a new street by the Vestry of Camberwell in 1883.

OLD NUN'S HEAD, No 15 NUNHEAD GREEN: The present pub was built in 1934 on the site of an inn reputedly licensed in the reign of Henry VIII. According to a local legend it was built on the site of a nunnery. The earliest record of an inn occupying this site is 1690, when it was described as 'The Nun's Head on the north east side of Peckham Rye, tea gardens'. In the 1760s it was called 'The Nun at Peckham Rye', a tavern and tea gardens, and by the early 20th century it was known by its present name.

The pub closed in December 2005, and following refurbishment and some minor alterations to the exterior, it reopened on 22nd September 2006.

Old Nun's Head

ONE TREE HILL PARK, BRENCHLEY GARDENS: Opened on the 7th August 1905 after a concerted campaign by local residents led by John Nisbet. The land on Honor Oak Hill had been enclosed by the owner of a golf club which caused a public outcry and riots. Over 30,000 people attended the opening ceremony.

PECKHAM RYE (EAST SIDE): Peckham Rye East extends from Scylla Road to Cheltenham Road. The Rye Hotel, No 31 Peckham Rye, occupies the site of the Rye House Tavern, first recorded here in 1819. Several early 19th century buildings exist on this side of the common including: Nos 141 to 153, formerly Rye Terrace, c.1827. In October 1903, a political murder took place here when two members of the Hentchakist Society, Aram Grigorian and Sigran Szmician, who were leaving their HQ at No 85 Peckham Rye, were shot dead by an Armenian revolutionary who had earlier murdered Sagatel Sagouni, the President of the Armenian Revolutionary Society, in Nunhead Grove. Both victims were Russians. Their assassin drew a second revolver from his pocket and shot himself.
    Arthur Saunders Rich (1807-65), cricketer, died at 'The Avenue', Nunhead Passage. He assisted in forming the East Surrey Cricket Club, Cam-

berwell in 1827. A left hand batsman and round-arm fast bowler, he first played at Lords in East Surrey v Marylebone in June 1830. **Stanley Hugh Coryton Roberts** (1889-1957) was born at No 71 'Avenue House', now covered by Howard Court. He was a son of Dr John Coryton Roberts (1841-1906), physician and surgeon. An outstanding figure in technical education, he founded the British School of Motoring in 1909 and was its first chairman. He went on to establish the College of Aeronautical and Automobile Engineering in 1924, and invented the Vestone gramophone. **The Revd Andrew Augustus Wild Drew** ((1837-1921), clergyman, lived at No 1 St George's Terrace, Peckham Rye, in the 1860s, and later at the vicarage No 123 Peckham Rye. He was born in Canada, the son of Admiral Andrew Drew. He founded, at his own expense, St Michael and All Angels, a mission church, in Linden Grove, and became the first vicar of St Antholin's in 1878, retiring in 1911. As the son of an admiral, he took a great interest in arctic exploration, and in 1875 he delivered a lecture on the 'forthcoming' Arctic Expedition. He had previously delivered lectures at the United Service Institution on armour clad ships and the training and working of heavy broadside guns. His father, **Admiral Andrew Drew RN** (1792-1878), lived and died at 'Glen Wood House' which stood at the corner of Rye Hill Park. A distinguished naval officer, he successfully defended Cape Coast Castle, West Africa, in charge of 160 men against an attack of thousands of Ashanti warriors. In 1837 he helped quell the Canadian rebellion by destroying an enemy ship which he sent flaming over the Niagara Falls. He was rewarded with the rank of Commodore of the Provincial Marine. **John Taylor** (d.1894), a Quaker stockbroker and treasurer of a home for destitute boys, lived at 'Sunbury'. His daughter, Elizabeth, later Dame Elizabeth Cadbury, also lived here. She married George Cadbury, the chocolate magnate and was very much involved in social work. **William Dowton JP** (1851-1913), local politician, lived and died at 'Park Lodge'. He was LCC member for Peckham from

James Buckland, a local magistrate, and his family outside 'Innesville' No 175 Peckham Rye East in 1907

1907 to 1910 and Mayor of Camberwell in 1912. **John Kirchner** (1814-91), artist and wood engraver, lived at Park Lodge Villa, Peckham Rye, in the 1860s. He engraved the plates for several of Edward Newman's books including *The Natural History of British Butterflies* (1874). From 1881 to his death in 1891 he was living at 'Bon Accord' No 183 Peckham Rye.

PECKHAM RYE (WEST SIDE): From Nigel Road (q.v.) to Dunstan's Road. Once known as Peckham Rye Road. Some of the houses on this side of the common date from the 1830s, including Nos 142, 152 to 166, and 200. Nos 40 to 48 and 202 to 212 were built in the 1840s.

Frank Ward (1919-91) a founder and later a rigorous opponent of the British Trotskyist movement, lived at No 204. His contributions to the revision of Labour Party policy won acclaim from Neil Kinnock (now Lord Kinnock), the former Labour leader. He was the author of *In Defence of Democratic Socialism* (1978). He spent the last years of his working life at Labour's HQ as information officer. **Henry Carl Schiller** (1807-71), writer and artist, lived and died at 'Manilla House' Peckham Rye. He was the author of *Christmas at the Grange*, a novel in two volumes, published under the name of Grey Anthony in 1845. His wife, **Annie Letitia Schiller** (d.1887), published *German National Cookery for English Kitchens* (1873). **John Nicholson** (1829-94), bibliographer, lived and died at No 228. He compiled the *Catalogue of Printed Books in the Library of the Hon Society of Lincoln's Inn*. **Vincent Figgins** (c.1767-1844), an eminent type-founder in Holborn, lived at No 1 Prospect Place, on which house is an oval plaque bearing its name in letters designed by him. He was also a Common Councillor for the ward of Farringdon Without in the City of London. **William Henry Hammond** (1802-85) auctioneer, lived at Prospect Place. He was the great-grandfather of the playwright Christopher Fry, author of *The Lady's Not For Burning*. A later resident, **Diana Ladas** (1913-2001), was headmistress of Heathfield School 1965-72. During the Second World War she worked in the Ministry of Economic Warfare and Board of Trade, and during the last months of peace she worked on the evacuation of Jewish refugees from Germany to Britain. From 1948 until 1950 she was on the staff of the British Information Service in New York. **Tom Hood** (1835-74), writer and artist, lived and died at No 92 'Gloucester Cottage'. He is best known as the editor of *Fun*, a satirical magazine. He also wrote poems and humorous novels and published *Tom Hood's Comic Annual* in 1867. **Sir Edmund Robbins** (1847-1922), journalist, lived and died at No 168. He was manager of the Press Association from 1880 to 1917, and vice-president of the Newspaper Press Fund in 1917. **Dame Elizabeth Cadbury DBE** (1858-1951), social reformer, was born at No 3 Elm Place, overlooking Rye Lake. **Commander George Millard RN** (1791-1870), lived at Warwick Place, a terrace that once adjoined the King's Arms pub. His ships were HMS *Canopus* and HM Yacht *Royal Sovereign*. He kept guard over Napoleon when he was imprisoned on St Helena. **Marian Richardson** (1830-72), poet, lived at Lancaster House. She and her husband John Richardson, were friends and supporters of the Italian patriot General Garibaldi. Her book *The Talk of the Household* (1865) includes poems on the American Civil War, Abraham Lincoln, and the death of Prince Albert. Of the 49 poems appearing in the book seven are related to the career of Garibaldi. The General visited the Richardsons at Peckham Rye in 1864. Their eldest son, **Joseph Hall Richardson** (1857-1945), General Manager of the Daily Telegraph, recalled in his memoirs his bitter disappointment at not being allowed to meet Garibaldi because he was suffering from a heavy cold at the time.

The west side of Peckham Rye in 1904

PECKHAM RYE COMMON: The common once belonged to Sir William Bowyer-Smyth (1814-83), Lord of the Manor of Camberwell Fryern. In 1865 he claimed absolute ownership of the common and wanted to build houses on it. The local inhabitants objected most strongly and took the case to the House of Commons. As a result, in 1869 the manorial rights were purchased by the Vestry of Camberwell and the common was saved for the people. Sir Walter Besant, the London historian, writing in 1898, described the Rye as 'a barren and dreary expanse of grass'. Barren it might have been - but dreary never! William Blake saw a crowd of angels on the common and in 1864 George Wombwell's Wild Beast Show took possession causing great concern to the local people, before being forced to move on. The Peckham Rye Band was the first to give Sunday music performances in a public open space in London, and the Rye was a popular meeting place for open air religious services. 'Unity Sunday' was celebrated annually on the first Sunday in July, the first occasion being in 1897. On this special day all the churches got together and thousands came to join in the prayers and singing. The Rye continues to be a valuable open space in crowded inner London.

Bandstand on the common. Damaged during the Second World War and demolished

*PECKHAM RYE CONGREGATIONAL CHURCH, LINDEN GROVE: Opened in Cemetery Road (now Linden Grove) in May 1857. It replaced a smaller building at Nunhead Green. The first pastor was the Revd Dr James Hiles Hitchens (1835-96) who was chaplain of Nunhead Cemetery. A popular lecturer, Dr Hitchens's historical and biographical talks attracted large audiences. He was succeeded in 1866 by the Revd Louis Herschell (1821-90). Born in Prussia, the son of distinguished Jewish parents, Herschell came to England as a boy and converted to Christianity. He was succeeded by the Revd John Chetwode Postans (1833-1905), who ministered here for almost 30 years. The church was demolished in the 1960s and replaced by a block of flats.

PECKHAM RYE PARK: The park occupies the former grounds of 'Homestall' also known as 'Peckham Farm'. In 1892 the last owner, Alfred Stevens, a Camberwell vestryman, sold the farm and its buildings to the Metropolitan Board of Works (forerunner of the LCC) for £51,000. The 50 acre park was opened to the public in 1894. It is now owned by

Southwark Council and is managed by the council and the Friends of Peckham Rye Park. It has recently been restored with money from the Heritage Lottery Fund.

Peckham Rye Park in the snow c.1904. Note the whalebone wishing arch

PECKHAM RYE BAPTIST TABERNACLE, NIGEL ROAD: Opened by the Revd Dr Charles Haddon Spurgeon (1834-1892) on Good Friday 1891. The tabernacle was damaged during the Second World War. A decreasing congregation required a smaller church which opened behind the old one in 1963. The Victorian building was demolished in 1970.

PECKHAM RYE SCHOOL, WHORLTON ROAD: Originally opened in 1884 by the School Board for London as an elementary school. Part of the school was used as a secondary school in the 1960s and was known as the Samuel Pepys annexe.

PECKHAM SOCIETY, THE: Founded in 1975 as the amenity society for Peckham and Nunhead, it covers the London SE15 postal district.

*PHILIP ROAD, PECKHAM RYE: Philip Road was laid out in the late 1860s between Peckham Rye and Albert Road (Consort Road) on land owned by the de Crespigny family. It was named after Philip Champion de Crespigny, and was adopted by the Vestry of Camberwell in 1873 and 1877. Only a small section of the street now remains renamed Philip Walk (q.v.) in the late 1970s. The remainder, leading to Consort Road, disappeared when the Consort Estate was built in the late 1970s.

PHILIP WALK: Pedestrian walkway on the Consort Estate built c.1978.

PIERMONT GREEN, PECKHAM RYE: A part of Peckham Rye now in the East Dulwich, London SE22, postal district.

PILKINGTON ROAD: Keating Road until 1878 when it was taken over by the Vestry of Camberwell. Perhaps named after Sir Thomas Pilkington (1773-1811), father-in-law to Sir John Tyssen Tyrrell. Occupants in 1881 included two stonemasons, an umbrella maker and a bank clerk.

*POPLARS, THE, PECKHAM RYE: This house stood at the corner of Nunhead Lane and Peckham Rye. In the 1870s it housed a ladies' school run by Emily and Louisa Groves, and by 1900 it was an orphanage, and later a dolls hospital. In the 1930s and 1940s it was occupied by Thompson's Corset Factory (q.v.). It was destroyed by a VI flying bomb in 1944 which killed 23 people. The site is now covered by Glover House built 1950/51.

POST OFFICES: Nunhead's first post-office opened at the corner of Nunhead Grove and Nunhead Lane in the 1870s. Samuel Green (1842-1907) was the first sub-postmaster. The office was relocated to No 38 Nunhead Green in 1998 and closed down in 2000. Post-offices were also situated in Ivydale and Cheltenham roads, both of which have since closed. The last remaining post-office is located in Gibbon Road near Nunhead Station, and is currently under threat of closure by Post Office Ltd and the government. The pillar box at Nunhead Green bears the cipher of Edward VIII who abdicated in 1936,

PRINCE ALBERT, No 119 CONSORT ROAD: This Victorian pub was built at the corner of Sturdy and Albert (now Consort) roads. It was renamed 'The Shergar' after the 1981 Derby winner who was kidnapped and disappeared without trace. Its last pub name was 'The Spotted Frog'. It is now 'The Frog on the Green' a popular delicatessen.

PRIORY COURT, No 1 CHELTENHAM ROAD, NEWLANDS: A small housing estate built by Southwark Council between 1972 and 1976. It covers the site of Priory Villas, destroyed by a VI flying bomb in 1944. The site was occupied by prefabricated houses until 1972.

PYROTECHNIST'S ARMS, No 39 NUNHEAD GREEN: An unusual name for a pub. It was built in the late 1860s near the firework manufactory of Charles Thomas Brock, the famous pyrotechnist, who made fireworks at Nunhead from the early 1860s until 1875.

The Pyrotechnist's Arms in the 1970s

*RAILWAY TAVERN, No 66 GIBBON ROAD: A Victorian pub so-named because it was built close to Nunhead Railway Station. It was demolished in 2004, and the site is now covered by a block of flats. At the time of writing the pub sign still stands at the corner of Gibbon Road and Kimberley Avenue. The tavern was a music hall from 1874 to 1891.

*RED HOUSE, No 218 PECKHAM RYE: Charles Burls (1814-96) lived here until his death. He was secretary of the London Cemetery Company and a guardian of the poor. Rye Court Estate (q.v.) was built on the site in the 1950s.
   Sir Edwin Grant Burls CSI ((1844-1926), of the India Office, and **Charles William Burls** (1847-1923), cricketer, who played for Surrey CCC between 1873 and 1880, were born here. They were sons of Charles Burls.

REYNOLDS ROAD, NEWLANDS: Pancras Road until October 1891. Adopted by the Vestry of Camberwell in 1889, and named after John Cook Reynolds (1816-1893), civil engineer. Reynolds was highways surveyor to the Vestry of Camberwell in 1856. He personally supervised over 50 miles of sewage and drainage works throughout the parish. A VI flying bomb came down here in 1944 destroying many houses. Prefabs were built on the site in 1946 and these were replaced by the Priory Court Estate (q.v.) in 1976.

ROSENTHORPE ROAD, WAVERLEY PARK: This road was laid out by Edward Yates in 1882 and was adopted by the Vestry of Lewisham in 1898. The origin of the name is unknown. Thorpe means farmhouse or homestead. Perhaps Rosen's Farm?

ROYAL ARSENAL CO-OPERATIVE STORE, NUNHEAD: A single storey building erected in 1928 from the designs of H G W Ackroyd. It occupies the site of a large house and surgery belonging to Dr Johnstone. The store was closed in the 1980s and is now occupied by several retailers.

Royal Arsenal Co-operative Stores, Nunhead Branch, in 1974

*ROYAL ARSENAL CO-OPERATIVE STORE, PECKHAM RYE: Co-operative House was built in 1932 to the designs of H G W Ackroyd. Above the store was a ballroom which was a popular rendezvous for teenagers between the 1940s and 1960s. The store was demolished in 2005 and a block of flats bearing the same name now occupies the site.

RUSSELL COURT, HEATON ROAD: A sheltered housing development built at the corner site of Heaton and Copeland roads in 1979-80. It perpetuates the name of Russell Road, now Blackpool Road.

RYE APARTMENTS: The post-war King's Arms pub (q.v.), later renamed King's on the Rye. It was converted to flats in 2000.

RYE COURT, PECKHAM RYE: Three blocks of three storey flats built in the 1950s on the site of the Red House (q.v.). The flats were originally built to accommodate policemen and policewomen and their families.

RYE HILL PARK, PECKHAM RYE: Rye Hill Park occupies a hill on the east side of Peckham Rye Common. It appears as Rye Hill Villas on maps in the 1860s, but wasn't adopted by the Vestry of Camberwell until 1883. Residents in 1881 included: a civil engineer, a wine merchant, a stockbroker, a solicitor, and a West India merchant. Most families employed a domestic servant. On the 27th June 1944 a VI flying bomb came down destroying many houses.
    Sir George Thomas Livesey (1834-1908), President of the South Metropolitan Gas Company, lived at Rye Hill Park in the 1860s. He was a supporter of many good causes and presented the people of Camberwell with their first public library in 1891.

RYE HILL ESTATE, PECKHAM RYE: Built by the London County Council in 1936 on land previously occupied by big houses with long gardens. The estate was extended in the 1960s. The original blocks were named after rivers. [Sherwood].

RYE HOTEL, No 31 PECKHAM RYE: Originally known as 'Rye House' and later as the 'Rye House Hotel'. A public house has been on this same site since at least 1819. Robert Proctor Tagg was 'mine host' from 1829 to his death in 1859, at the age of 64. He is buried in Nunhead Cemetery. The pub was rebuilt between the two World Wars.

RYE ROAD, NEWLANDS: Rye was the popular name for Peckham Rye Common. Adopted by Camberwell Borough Council in 1900.

RYEVIEW, No 110 PECKHAM RYE (WEST SIDE): Overlooking Peckham Rye Common. A small housing development built in the 1980s close to the site of the Peckham Rye branch of Westminster Bank Ltd.

ST ANTHOLIN'S, CARDEN ROAD: St Antholin's replaced the temporary iron church of St Michael and All Angels, Linden Grove. Construction began in 1877, and it was consecrated on 11th May 1878. The architect was Ewan Christian (1814-1895). Two bells and the altar piece from the demolished Wren church of St Antholin's, Watling Street, were brought here. Improvement works were carried out by Martin Travers in 1939. The church was badly damaged by fire-bombs in 1940, and reconstructed and rededicated in 1957.

ST ANTONY'S CHURCH, CARDEN ROAD: Built as St Antholin's (q.v.) in 1878, it was badly damaged by fire bombs in December 1940. The Lady Chapel was used for christenings and marriages while awaiting reconstruction. The church was rebuilt by Laurence King, and reopened and rededicated to St Antony by the Bishop of Southwark on 12th October 1957. The parish of St Antony was united with St Silas (q.v.) in 1990, and services were held in both churches, until St Antony with St Silas opened in Ivydale Road in 2003. The building is now used by the Lighthouse Cathedral.

St Antony's Church, formerly St Antholin's and now the Lighthouse Cathedral, pictured here in the 1970s

ST ANTONY WITH ST SILAS, IVYDALE ROAD: Built on the island site of St Silas' to the designs of Oliver West and John Scott, and consecrated by the Bishop of Woolwich on Saturday 26th April, 2003.

ST ASAPH ROAD: Laid out in the 1890s. Only a small section of this street, from Ivydale Road to the railway bridge, lay in the Metropolitan Borough of Camberwell (now the London Borough of Southwark). The remainder, originally in the Metropolitan Borough of Deptford, is now in the London Borough of Lewisham. The Nunhead section was adopted by Camberwell Borough Council in 1907. Possibly named after St Asaph, a place in North Wales.

ST MARY'S CHURCH HALL, ST MARY'S ROAD: The foundation stone was laid by Mrs Alfred Stevens of Homestall Farm, Peckham Rye, and the hall was opened in 1890.

St Mary Magdalene's Church 1905

ST MARY MAGDALENE'S CHURCH, ST MARY'S ROAD: The original church was built on a plot of land known as the Ducks' Nest, given by William Edmonds of New Cross. It was built in 1839-41 and consecrated by the Bishop of Winchester in 1841. The architect was Robert Palmer Browne (c.1802-1872). A baptistery and apse were added in 1910 by Arthur Heron Ryan-Tenison (1861-1930). The church was badly damaged by a landmine in September 1940. The remains of the old church were demolished and a new church was built on the site in 1961-2. It was consecrated on the 3rd November 1962. The architects were Potter and Hare.

ST MARY MAGDALENE'S SCHOOL, GODMAN ROAD: A Church of England school was erected here in 1856, and was the first purpose built school in the district. Local children attended classes at St Mary Magdalene's Church until the school was built. A girls' school was added in 1894. A new school was built nearby in the early 2000s, and the old schools, much altered, were converted into housing units in 2005.

St Mary Magdalene's Church of England School in 1973

ST MARY'S ROAD: Laid out in the late 1830s connecting Deptford Lane (now Queen's Road, Peckham) with Nunhead and St Mary Magdalene's Church. The section of road from the church to Evelina Road was taken over as a new street by the Vestry of Camberwell in 1866. The Pioneer Health Centre (known locally as the Glass House) was built in 1935 to fulfil the requirements of Dr Scott Williamson for the 'Peckham Experiment' a radical health scheme. The centre closed during the Second World War and reopened in 1946, only to close in 1950 through lack of funds. 'R E Sassoon House' opposite St Mary Magdalene's Church, was designed by Maxwell Fry in 1932, and given to the Pioneer Health Centre by Mrs Meyer Sassoon in memory of her son.

Revd Thomas Goss MA (1836-98), vicar of St Mary Magdalene's Church from 1893 to death, lived at No 22. **Alderman Robert Lyon** (1850-1904), local politician, lived at No 36. He was the member for Peckham of the first London County Council and a member of the first Metropolitan Water Board. **Revd Thomas Cole** (1822-1902) lived at No 44. He was founder and first pastor of Nunhead Baptist Chapel (q.v.). **George Colwell Oke** (1821-74), eminent legal writer, lived and died at Rosedale, St Mary's Road. The author of many legal works, he was also Chief Clerk to the Lord Mayor of London from 1864 to death.

ST MICHAEL AND ALL ANGELS, NUNHEAD: A temporary mission church was erected in Linden Grove in 1866 at the expense of the Revd Andrew Augustus Wild Drew (1837-1921), and was used until St Antholin's Church (q.v.) was built in 1878.

ST PAUL'S CHURCH, CONSORT ROAD: Built as a mission church to serve the increasing population of St Mary Magdalene's parish. The foundation stone was laid by Mrs Alfred Stevens of Homestall Farm, Peckham Rye. The church was consecrated by the Bishop of Southwark on 5th January 1907. The space beneath the church was known as the Hooper Memorial Hall. It is now used by the 'Tent of Testimonies' an independent church.

St Paul's Church in 1973

*ST SILAS' CHURCH, IVYDALE ROAD: This church was built for the residents of the Waverley Park Estate (q.v.). Building began in 1902, and it consecrated on 17th October 1903. The congregation originally met in a shop in Ivydale Road before the Waverley Park Mission Hall (q.v.) was built. The new church, in the 15th century style, was designed by John Edward Knight Cutts (1847-1938) and his brother, John Priston Cutts (1854-1935). The first stone was laid on All Saints Day, 1st November 1902, but the church wasn't completed until 1913. Edward Yates (1838-1907), the developer of the estate, contributed to the building fund and provided the island site. He was commemorated by a tablet set into the wall of the church. The church suffered some bomb damage during the Second World War, which possibly contributed to its unsafe condition. In the 1990s it was decided it couldn't be restored. A farewell service was held in a marquee outside the church in May 2001. The church was demolished in July and August 2001, and was replaced by St Antony with St Silas Church (q.v.) in 2003.

St Silas's Church 1974. Demolished 2001

ST THOMAS THE APOSTLE RC CHURCH, EVELINA ROAD: St Thomas the Apostle was opened in November 1905 to provide a place of worship for Nunhead's Roman Catholics. A school associated with this church was built in 1965 in Hollydale Road on the site of a convent.

ST THOMAS THE APOSTLE RC COLLEGE, HOLLYDALE ROAD: Opened in 1965 as St Thomas the Apostle School on the site of the Marist Convent and a house known as 'The Retreat'.

SAILOR PRINCE, No 86 GORDON ROAD: A Victorian pub dating from the 1870s since converted into flats.

SALISBURY TERRACE, BARSET ROAD: Built 1981-82. The original Salisbury Terrace was part of Barset Road until June 1897 when the name was abolished, and the terrace was renumbered as part of the street.

SALVATION ARMY CITADEL: The first Nunhead Salvation Army Citadel opened in Gordon Road in 1891 and was badly damaged by bombs during the Blitz in 1940. A new Citadel was built on the same site opened by General Wilfred Kitching (d.1970) in February 1960. Henry Hall OBE (1898-1989), the well-known dance band leader, learned to play the cornet and concertina here. He was born in Peckham and his parents were members of the Nunhead SA.

Turret House, Nunhead Green, mid-19th century

SALVATION ARMY HALL: This building backs on to the Salvation Army Citadel in Gordon Road. It dates from 1956 and replaced an earlier building which was destroyed by bombs in 1940. The hall occupies the site of 'Turret House'.

SARTOR ROAD, NEWLANDS: Laid out in the 1860s on the south side of Nunhead Hill, and adopted by the Vestry of Camberwell in 1898. J A Dunn, a tailor, made an application for this road to be laid out in 1863, and resided in one of the cottages. Sartor is Latin for tailor. [Beasley].

Monks Cottages, Scylla Road, awaiting restoration in 1974

SCYLLA ROAD: Originally a part of Nunhead Passage and Sherlock Road until 1878. It was adopted by the Vestry of Camberwell in stages: from Nunhead Green to Albert Road (now Consort Road) in 1873; from Peckham Rye to Claude Road in 1878; and from Claude Road to the posts by Beeston House in 1884. The remainder was taken over by Camberwell Borough Council in 1926. Scylla Road occupies former de Crespigny land, and is named after HMS Scylla, a ship commanded by Captain Augustus James de Crespigny RN, who died aboard the vessel in 1826, having served under Admiral Lord Nelson. A VI flying bomb came down at the junction with Claude Road (q.v.) in 1944 destroying several houses and damaging many more.

Vane Ireton Shaftesbury St John (1839-1911), a pioneer of boys' books, lived at No 53. He was a younger brother of Sir Spenser Buckingham St John, and wrote many books for boys. He also founded and edited the journal *Boys of England*. He was twice married and fathered 17 children. **Sir Godfrey Way Mitchell** (1891-1982), civil engineer and entrepreneur, was born at No

54. In 1919 he took over a small insolvent masonry business in Hammersmith founded by George Wimpey. He enlarged the business and, trading under the name of George Wimpey & Co Ltd, became one of the largest house builders in the world. **Denis Bond** (1952 -) children's writer and actor, lived with his parents in Scylla Road as a child (near the Old Nun's Head). He first worked as an actor on stage and TV appearing in *The Bill* and *Keeping Up Appearances* before becoming a teacher. He wrote children's programmes for TV including *Rainbow* and *The Munch Bunch*. His first book *Dagon Comes Down to Earth* was published in 1983, and his latest *Pop Rivals* in 2004.

SELDEN ROAD: Laid out in the late 1860s. Boundary changes in 1900 divided the road between the Metropolitan Borough of Camberwell (now Southwark) and the Metropolitan Borough of Deptford (now Lewisham). It was taken over as a new street by resolution of the Vestry of Camberwell in 1889. Occupants in 1881 included: a gunsmith, a post office sorter, a railway guard and railway signalman, and an estate agent. In 1949 Messrs Jeune and Heyman founded J & H Transport Services at No 11a with just one old lorry. By 1960 they owned over 100 vehicles had 15 branches throughout the UK. Mr Heyman died in 1962 and the firm removed to Deptford.

Harry Munro (1830-76), second son of Sir Charles Munro, 9th baronet of Foulis, lived at No 2a (demolished).

J & H Transport started their business in Selden Road in the late 1940s

SENATE STREET: Boundary road shared by Camberwell (now Southwark) and Deptford (now Lewisham). Originally wholly in the parish of St Giles, Camberwell, it was taken over by the Vestry of Camberwell in 1889. Its occupants in 1881 included: a Chelsea pensioner, a horse keeper, a brick maker and a jobbing labourer. Many houses were destroyed when a VI flying bomb came down here in 1944.

SHELLEY CLOSE, GORDON ROAD: A small housing development c.1989, built on vacant land behind houses. Named after the poet Percy Bysshe Shelley. [Beasley].

*SOLOMON'S LANE, PECKHAM RYE: A footway that once led from the east side of Peckham Rye to a large house called 'The Vineries'. The lane disappeared when the Rye Hill Estate was built in the 1930s. A fingerpost pointing to 'The Vineries' still existed in the 1960s.

SOLOMON'S PASSAGE, PECKHAM RYE: Part road and part footpath connecting Peckham Rye East with Carden Road and Forester Road. Originally a footpath from Peckham Rye to Cemetery Road, now Linden Grove. It gets its name from Israel Solomon, a market gardener, whose house, Pineapple Lodge, once adjoined Solomon's Passage.

SOMERTON ROAD, PECKHAM RYE: Taken over as a new street by the Vestry of Camberwell in 1899. Named after Somerton Lodge, one of several large houses on Peckham Rye.

STANBURY ROAD: Taken over as a new street by the Vestry of Camberwell in 1879. On the 23rd June 1944 a VI flying bomb came down between Stanbury and Hollydale roads killing two people and destroying many houses.

*STAR OF INDIA, GORDON ROAD: A Victorian pub built at the corner of Brayard's and Gordon roads in the 1870s. It was damaged by arsonists and demolished in September 1998. The site, having remained vacant for nine years, is now being built on.

STRAKER'S ROAD, PECKHAM RYE: Originally a thoroughfare cutting across Peckham Rye Common. It has been closed to through traffic since the Second World War, and is now only an access road to the park.

Samuel Straker (d.1874), a Camberwell vestryman and stationer in the City of London, lived at 'Sunnyside', a large house on Straker's Road. **Alderman Samuel Tothill Martin** (1852-1910), a later resident, was Mayor of Camberwell in 1909.

STUART ROAD, NEWLANDS: Named after Stuart Villas, one of several terraces lining the road. Adopted by the Vestry of Camberwell between 1886 and 1898. Bredinghurst School (opened 1948) occupies a large house built in 1874. It was originally used as a children's home by the Camberwell Poor Law Union. On the 1st July 1944, a VI flying bomb came down at the junction of Stuart and Reynolds roads demolishing 16 houses and claiming 17 lives. Prefabs were built on the site in 1946 and these were replaced by Priory Court Estate (q.v.) in 1976.

STURDY ROAD: Laid out in the mid-1860s and taken over by the Vestry of Camberwell in 1869. The terraced houses on the south side were demolished in the 1970s to create an open space, now known as Dr Harold Moody Park. The residents in 1881 included: several labourers, a watchmaker and a police constable. The road is probably named after Daniel Sturdy, a former owner of the site. [Sherwood].

SURREY ROAD, NEWLANDS: Laid out in the 1890s, and taken over as a new street by the Vestry of Camberwell in 1899.

SWISS TAVERN, No 44 LAUSANNE ROAD: A pub was first built here in the 1870s and was named in association with the street in which it was built. Lausanne is in Switzerland.

SYMONS CLOSE, EVELINA ROAD: A modern block of flats built on the site of Nunhead Petrol Station. It was originally the site of No 5 East Terrace, Evelina Road, where lived Charles Peace, a notorious burglar and murderer whose name became part of folk myth along with Robin Hood and Dick Turpin. He was executed by hanging in 1879. The house in which he lived for just two years was destroyed during an air raid in 1941.

TAPPESFIELD ROAD: Laid out in the late 1870s and taken over as a new street by the Vestry of Camberwell in 1882. Named after Henry Tappesfield, who married Susan Muschamp of Peckham. [Blanch].

*THOMPSON'S CORSET FACTORY, No 105 PECKHAM RYE: This factory occupied a large house at the corner of Nunhead Lane in the 1930s and 1940s. It was destroyed by a VI flying bomb on 22nd June 1944, killing 15 girl workers aged between 15 and 20. The eventual death toll was 23, and many more persons were injured. The house, originally known as 'The Poplars' (q.v.) was once a girls' school and later a dolls' hospital. The site is now occupied by Glover House.

THORN TERRACE, NUNHEAD GROVE: A late Victorian terrace, one of several in Nunhead Grove.

TORRIDGE GARDENS, PECKHAM RYE: Laid out by the LCC as an extension to the Rye Hill Estate in 1958/59. Named after the River Torridge. All blocks of flats on this estate were named after rivers.

TRESCO ROAD: Laid out in the 1870s and adopted as a new street by the Vestry of Camberwell in 1882. At the 1881 census the residents included: a bookbinder, a civil engineer, a Chelsea Pensioner, a civil servant employed at Somerset House, and a master printer employing 9 men and three boys. At least 13 houses were unoccupied. Perhaps named after Tresco, one of the Scilly Isles. [Sherwood].
   Sir Thomas Wilson McAra JP (1864-1942), compositor, lived at No 24 in the 1920s. He was a former chairman of the Technical Committee, London Newspaper Proprietors' Association. **Olive Mary Shapley** (1910-99), broadcaster, was born at No 10. In 1934 she obtained a post with BBC radio organising *Children's Hour*. In 1949 she presented *Woman's Hour* and was associated with the programme for over 20 years. She also worked as a TV presenter in London, before switching to production in 1959. She retired in 1973.

TROY TOWN, PECKHAM RYE: Originally a cluster of cottages on the west side of Peckham Rye, near the White Horse Tavern. The name 'Troy Town' suggests a maze i.e. a maze of streets. Occupants in 1881 included: several laundresses, a launderer, an unemployed ostler and several labourers.

*TYRRELL ARMS, No 25 NUNHEAD LANE: The original Victorian pub was destroyed during the Second World War. A new pub, with the same name, was built on the site in the 1960s and demolished in 2001. A block of flats now occupies the site.

*VIVIAN GROVE: Vivian Road until February 1938. Laid out in the early 1870s on land formerly owned by the de Crespignys of Camberwell, and adopted by the Vestry of Camberwell in 1876. Named after Sir Richard Hussey (1775-1842), 1st Baron Vivian, who married Eliza, daughter of Philip Champion de Crespigny in 1804. The street was demolished in the 1970s to make way for the Consort Estate. In 1881 the residents included: several clerks, a traveller and a dressmaker.

A derelict Vivian Grove awaiting demolition in 1974

*VIVIAN HOTEL, 11 PHILIP TERRACE, PHILIP ROAD: Damaged by bombs during the Second World War, it was demolished in the 1970s to make way for the Consort Estate. It occupied land originally owned by the de Crespigny's, and commemorated Baron Vivian (1775-1842), brother-in-law to Sir Claude Champion de Crespigny.

VIVIAN SQUARE: Part of Southwark Council's Consort Estate laid out in the late 1970s. Close to the site of Vivian Grove (q.v.).

WATER MEWS: Built on the site of the covered reservoirs in Linden Grove in the 1990s.

WAVENEY AVENUE, PECKHAM RYE: This street was laid out in the 1890s. Only 19 houses had been built on the street by 1896. It was taken over as a new street by the Vestry of Camberwell in 1897.

WAVERLEY ARMS, No 202 IVYDALE ROAD: Built in the 1880s on the Waverley Park Estate by the developer Edward Yates. No other pubs were allowed on his estate.

WAVERLEY PARK ESTATE, NUNHEAD: The Waverley Park Estate was laid out by Edward Yates (1838-1907), a speculative builder and property developer, between 1877 and 1895, on four fields of about 19 acres lying south and east of Nunhead Cemetery. It mainly encompasses Ivydale (q.v.), Limesford (q.v.) and Athenlay (q.v.) roads. Yates bought the freehold of the land for £6,300, and in 1884 leased another two parcels of land from the Trustees of Christ's Hospital. Meanwhile, he bought around 18 acres adjoining the Christ's Hospital land, and purchased the grounds of 'The Vista', about six acres on the south side of Nunhead Cemetery, from Mrs Nancy Scully. By 1888 'The Waverley Arms' had been built on Ivydale Road together with a temporary school of the London School Board. A permanent school was built in 1893. Several shops and a post-office were also built. Yates contributed towards the building of St Silas Church and a small Methodist chapel at Nos 149-159 Ivydale Road. Yates lived at No 56 Half Moon Lane, Dulwich from c.1890, and died at Finchingfield, Essex in April 1907. He is buried in West Norwood Cemetery.

WAVERLEY PARK METHODIST CHURCH, IVYDALE ROAD: This church originally belonged to the Methodist New Connexion. Edward Yates, the developer of the estate, contributed £50 to the building fund. It was built in 1896 and became a United Methodist Church in 1907. It was known as Waverley Park Methodist Church after the union of the Methodist churches in 1932. The last service was held in 1947, and the building became an organ factory and was later used by electrical engineers. It became the meeting place of the Peckham Seventh Day Adventists in 1986.

*WAVERLEY PARK MISSION HALL, INVERTON ROAD: The foundation stone was laid by a Major Scriven on the 5th October 1895. The Revd John Robinson MA was the first curate-in-charge. The hall was used as a temporary church by the Anglicans of the Waverley Park Estate pending the opening of St Silas's Church in 1903. Thereafter it was used as their church hall. It was burnt down by arsonists in July 2005.

WAVERLEY SCHOOL, HOMESTALL ROAD: Created in 1978 by merging Honor Oak Girls School (q.v.) with Friern Road Secondary Modern Girls School, to form a new comprehensive. It has since been extended and is now known as the Harris Academy.

*WAXED PAPERS LTD, NUNHEAD LANE: Until 1962 there were three paper mills behind and to the west of the Nunhead bus garage (q.v.), known as the Star, Acme and Victory. Waxed Papers Ltd was formed in 1923 by the amalgamation of the Anglo-Canadian Waxed Paper Company of Watford, and George Church of Nunhead. George Church founded the Star Paper Mills at 18A Nunhead Lane in the early years of the 20th century. The firm pioneered the conversion of paper for wrapping food, specialising in bread and sweet wrappers. Many local families were employed by the firm, whose products were exported to all parts of the world. The business was taken over by Wiggins Teape Ltd and production transferred to Kenton, Middlesex in 1962. Banfield Road (q.v.) now occupies the site.

Waxed Papers Limited - paper mills and warehouses in 1962

WELLINGTON MEWS, PECKHAM RYE: A small modern housing development on the west side of the Rye.

WHITE HORSE, No 20 PECKHAM RYE: A public house has occupied this site since before 1810. The present building dates from the 1930s.

The 'Old White Horse' and the Peckham Rye Tabernacle (right) in 1905

WHORLTON ROAD, PECKHAM RYE: Taken over as a new street by the Vestry of Camberwell in 1897.

WILLIAMSON COURT, PECKHAM RYE: Built in recent years on the site of Deanes pram factory.

WROXTON ROAD: Taken over as a new street by the Vestry of Camberwell in 1881. Residents at that time included: a master plumber, a compositor, a pocket book maker and an artist.

ZETLAND TERRACE, NUNHEAD GREEN: This name was abolished in 1889 and the terrace was renumbered Nos 10-20 Nunhead Green. The terrace was converted into flats by Southwark Council in the mid-

1970s, and won the Royal Institute of Chartered Surveyors/Times Conservation award in 1976.

George Ruthven (1816-1871) lived here in the 1860s. He was Assistant Secretary to the Great Indian Peninsular Railway Company, and friend and father-in-law to James (later Sir James) Augustus Murray, lexicographer, compiler of the first Oxford English Dictionary, who lived nearby at Beaufort Terrace, Nunhead Lane. **Dr John Coryton Roberts** (1841-1906), physician and surgeon, had his surgery here. He was physician to the Metropolitan Beer and Wine Sellers Society, and public vaccinator for south Peckham.

Nos 10-20 Nunhead Green, formerly Zetland Terrace, undergoing restoration in the 1970s. The doorway between the terrace and Harry Birkett's betting office, was once known as the 'Marble Arch' and led to Cemetery Cottages (demolished).

BIBLIOGRAPHY
including publications consulted and books recommended for further reading.

John D Beasley: *The Story of Peckham* (Southwark Council, 1976)
John D Beasley: *Who was Who in Peckham* (Chener Books, 1985)
John D Beasley: *Origin of Names in Peckham & Nunhead* (South Riding Press, 1993)
John D Beasley: *Peckham Rye Park 1894-1994* (South Riding Press, 1994)
John D Beasley: *Peckham & Nunhead Churches* (South Riding Press, 1995)
John D Beasley: *Peckham & Nunhead* (Chalford Publishing Co Ltd, 1995)
John D Beasley: *Peckham Rye Park Centenary* (South Riding Press, 1995)
John D Beasley: *Transport in Peckham & Nunhead* (South Riding Press, 1997)
John D Beasley: *The Story of Peckham & Nunhead* (Southwark Council, 1999)
John D Beasley: *Peckham & Nunhead Remembered* (Tempus Publishing, 2000)

Walter George Bell: *Where London Sleeps* (John Lane the Bodley Head, 1926)
Sir Walter Besant: *London South of the Thames* (Adam & Charles Black, 1912)
Sir Walter Besant: *South London* (Chatto and Windus, 1899, reprinted 1912)
Mick Blakeman: *Nunhead Football Club 1888-1949* (Yore Publications, 2000)
William Harnett Blanch: *Ye Parish of Camerwell* (E W Allen, 1875)
Mary Boast: *Southwark - A London Borough* (Southwark Council, 1970)
Stephen Bourne: *Speak of me as I am - The Black presence in Southwark since 1600* (Southwark Council 2005)
Brayley and Britton: *A Topographical History of Surrey* (G Willis, Covent Garden,1850)
Alan St H Brock: *A History of Fireworks* (George G Harrap, 1949)
Michèle Louise Burford: *Camberwell - including Dulwich, Peckham and Nunhead: streets and terraces etc, renamed and renumbered 1856-1953* (manuscript, 2001)
Camberwell Vestry 37th Annual Report of the Parish of Camberwell (1893)
Camberwell Golden Jubilee Official Handbook (Camberwell Borough Council, 1950)
Camberwell - The Official Guide, 8th edition (Camberwell Borough Council, 1953)
Street List (Camberwell Borough Council, 1954)
Tim Charlesworth: *The Architecture of Peckham* (Chener Books, 1988)
Basil Clarke: *The Parish Churches of London* (B T Batsford, 1966)
Harold P Clunn: *London Marches On* (The Caen Press, 1947)
Michael Counsell (ed): *The Story of the One Tree Agitation by Councillor John Nisbet* (reprinted and published by Michael Counsell, 1997)
James Stevens Curl: *Nunhead Cemetery London* (Ancient Monument Society, 1977)
H J Dyos: *A Victorian Suburb* (Leicester University Press, 1961)
John Field: *Place Names of Greater London* (BT Batsford, 1980)
Christopher Hibbert & Ben Weinreb (eds): *The London Encyclopaedia* (Macmillan, 1983)
Stephen Humphrey: *Camberwell, Dulwich & Peckham* (Sutton Publishing, 1996)
William Kent: *Encyclopaedia of London* (J M Dent and Sons, 1937)
List of Principal Streets in London showing Initials of the Postal District and Number of the Office of Delivery (General Post Office, March 1917)
London Borough of Southwark Official Guide (Southwark Council 1970)
Peter Marcan: *Visions of Southwark* (Peter Marcan Publications, 1997)
H E Malden (ed): *The Victoria History of the County of Surrey*, volume 6 (1912, reprinted 1967 by University of London)
Arthur Mee: *Mee's London* (Hodder and Staunton, 1946)
A D Mills: *Dictionary of London Place Names* (Oxford University Press, 2001)
K M Elisabeth Murray: *Caught in the Web of Words - James Murray and the Oxford English Dictionary* (Oxford University Press, 1979)
Sam Price Myers: *London South of the River* (Paul Elek, 1949)
Joan Read: *Lewisham Street Names and their Origins before 1965* (Joan Read, 1990)
Ann Saunders (ed): *London County Council Bomb Damage Maps 1939-1945* (London Topographical Society, 2005)
William Saunders: *History of the First London County Council* (National Press, 1892)
L Sherwood: *Camberwell Place and Street Names and their Origin* (Camberwell, 1964)
R W Shields: *Peckham Rye Baptist Tabernacle* (Peckham Rye Tabernacle, 1948)

Roger Smith: *Centenary Viewpoint - St Antony's Nunhead* (St Antony's, 1978)
Jes Steele (ed): *The Streets of London - The Booth Notebooks, South East* (Deptford Forum Publishing, 1997)
Tim and Carol Stevenson (eds): *Short Guide to Nunhead Cemetery* (FONC, 2003)
Gwyneth Stokes (ed): *Nunhead Cemetery - An Illustrated Guide* (FONC, 1988)
Richard Tames: *Dulwich and Camberwell Past with Peckham* (Historical Publications, 1997)
Edward Walford: *Old and New London - Southern Suburbs* Vol VI (Cassell, c.1878)
Olive M Walker: *A Tour of Camberwell* (H H Greaves, 1954)
David Ward: *King of the Lags - The Story of Charles Peace* (Souvenir Press, 1989)
Harry Williams: *South London* (Robert Hale, 1949)
Ron Woollacott: *Nunhead Notables* (FONC, 1984)
Ron Woollacott: *More Nunhead Notables* (FONC, 1995)
Ron Woollacott: *A Historical Tour of Nunhead and Peckham Rye* (Maureen & Ron Woollacott, 1995)
Ron Woollacott: *Camberwell Old Cemetery* (M & R Woollacott, 2000)
Ron Woollacott: *Nun Green to Plow Garlick Hill* (M & R Woollacott, 2001)
Ron Woollacott: *Southwark's Burying Places* (M & R Woollacott, 2001)
Ron Woollacott: *Nunhead & Peckham Pubs* (M & R Woollacott, 2002)

Other sources: the Dictionary of National Biography, Modern English Biography, Who's Who (various years), local newspapers and parish magazines, old and new maps, street directories and census returns from 1841 to 1901.

A restored LGOC bus parked in the yard outside Nunhead Bus Garage. The rear of Brookstone Court is on the left and the flats in Nunhead Lane are in the background. The site is now covered by Banfield Road housing development.